A Fine Line

When Discipline Becomes Child Abuse

Dr. David A. Sabatino

 Human Services Institute
Bradenton, Florida

TAB **TAB BOOKS**
Blue Ridge Summit, PA

FIRST EDITION
FIRST PRINTING

Library of Congress Cataloging-in-Publication Data

Sabatino, David A.
    A fine line : when discipline becomes child abuse / by David A. Sabatino.
      p. cm.
   ISBN 0-8306-3366-9   ISBN 0-8306-3566-1 (pbk.)
    1. Discipline of children—United States. 2. Child abuse—United
States.
HQ770.4.S23   1990
649′.64—dc20
                  90-36459
                  CIP

TAB Books offers software for sale. For information and a catalog, please contact TAB Software Department, Blue Ridge Summit, PA 17294-0850.

Development Editor: Dr. Lee Marvin Joiner
Copy Editors: Pat Hammond and Pat Holliday
Acquisition Editor: Kim Tabor
Cover Photograph: Susan Riley, Harrisonburg, VA

Questions regarding the content of this book should be addressed to:

Human Services Institute, Inc.
P.O. Box 14610
Bradenton, FL 34280

This book is dedicated to parenting.

Contents

Acknowledgments

I am indebted to many people for their invaluable assistance in writing this book. Dr. Lee Marvin Joiner, Senior Editor, HSI/TAB-McGraw-Hill, Inc. and his staff, including Pat Hammond and Pat Holliday, have turned rough material into readable information. Their interest in this project, and talents, are clearly reflected in the final product.

The mountain of data and information collected from sources all over this country was provided by graduate assistants at both the University of West Virginia College of Graduate Studies and East Tennessee State University. This list includes Stacy Perry, Margaret Ralston, Cindy McIntosh, Kenneth Jarrett, and Katharine Middleton. To these colleagues I extend a special note of appreciation.

I am grateful for the help of the technological age secretaries who can not only work a word processor, but can work *on* a word processor. I have much to learn. This group of talented people includes Terri McFeature, Betty Rutherford, Marilyn Armentrout and Joan Cavender.

To my friends Dr. Robert Smith and Dr. Kay Porter, it was a pleasure to see your work with clients come alive in the chapters you have provided. It is you and the human service community who hold the line against those conditions that would destroy the human spirit.

Countless others read, edited, swore, and found materials. I cannot tell you the names of everyone in this group, but my friend, Ms. Oetjen, must have read each word at least four times.

This book exists because of all of you.

Introduction

Child abuse is ineffective parenting in the extreme. In writing *A Fine Line,* a book about where discipline ends and child abuse begins, I have tried to reach a wide range of readers. The practitioner working daily with domestic violence or child abuse and neglect will find that I offer a distinct viewpoint, one that is broader than most.

A Fine Line may appeal to those who do not work principally with abused children, but who are interested in children, especially family discipline. I have included historical material on punishment to help readers better understand where and how widely held beliefs about punishing children originated.

This is not a "cookbook" on parental intervention, nor a parent-training manual. I have concentrated on something more fundamental, parental attitudes. These attitudes determine parenting responses and serve as the guiding values for a society. A historical review and trend analysis of attitudes promoting good disciplinary and child management practices also is offered.

Another audience is educators, school counselors, and counselors in agencies serving families facing domestic violence. Counselors, child and family case workers, public and school health nurses, child and family therapists, and those who labor in protective shelters are concerned about effective interventions. For them, I offer therapeutic suggestions in each chapter. I believe that in deciding how to help families, the therapist must first examine parental values. Are these values socially responsive and do they support positive interactions? If not, new learning is in order. I have dedicated a chapter to Rational Behavior Therapy, an effective approach to parent education.

To assume that a community knows how to respond to domestic violence is similar to assuming that all parents have well-developed parenting skills. Parenting skills must be taught. I also believe it is extremely important for human service providers to promote changes in the community attitudes about discipline and child abuse. *A Fine Line* offers counselors and human service providers information for hastening change.

It has been my aspiration to offer parents, ministers, administrators of community agencies, and the concerned public a thought-provoking message about how our behavior as adults affects children as they learn values and decision-making skills. It is a crucial area of concern because the consequences of what we do today are transgenerational. Our children will employ our responses and solutions when they reach adulthood, teaching them, in turn, to their own children.

Child abuse will not stop by punishing its perpetrators any more than the war on drugs has stopped drug use. For one thing societal preoccupation with punishment sends the wrong message. Punishment does not teach new values and new decision-making skills. These skills must be taught by all agencies serving the public, from the police and courts to those shaping public policy.

CROSSING THE LINE

I have a driver's license and a hunting license in my wallet. Each time I purchase a gun I must complete a Federal Firearms Registration form declaring that I am not a substance abuser nor have I ever been a felon. If I have, I cannot obtain that weapon. I must register my car yearly. I must have it inspected. I cannot build on my lot without a permit. My life is even regulated to the extent that my dog must have a rabies shot each year and a dog tag, besides his rabies tag. Yes, my dog is registered too. I must take a test proving that I know the driving laws, and then demonstrate that I can drive, before I am permitted to operate a motor vehicle.

However, before I married, I did not take a test asking me to explain how much I knew about relationships, or loving, or being a husband. I have never taken a parenting test and, yet, I have spent over half my life attempting to accomplish that feat with no training except the observation of my father and selected men in my community. I am not unique. Parenting skills are presumed, not taught. The results are sometimes tragic.

Bob Smith (a pseudonym) is in a batterers' treatment group for adult males who are physically and emotionally violent with their loved ones. Mr. Smith was physically abused as a child. He has never been in jail, but he might well have been. He physically and emotionally abuses his wife, and, frequently, his children. He finds it difficult to think about how he should discipline his children. He cannot even decide which acceptable behaviors he wants them to display. He becomes paralyzed with anxiety over the subject and cannot talk, or even think, about it without a stress reaction. Therefore, he does not talk with his family about what he feels should be the rules for the home nor what is appropriate behavior. Lacking rules, he becomes upset.

Trying to avoid the truth, and his hopeless feelings of being a poor husband and father, he desensitizes his discomfort by drinking too much. Alcohol gives him the courage he needs to try to control what he believes are the trials of parenthood aimed directly at him. In short, he personalizes and resents his children's and spouse's behaviors.

He feels inadequate as a father because he cannot establish and communicate appropriate rules of conduct and behavior to his household. He waits until things have gone too far. Then he becomes angry. He punishes the children, frequently beating them with his fists, hitting them in the face and stomach until they must be taken to the emergency room. They are afraid to report him, so they deny that their injuries were inflicted by their father.

Mr. Smith always feels badly about losing control of his temper and striking his children. As is common in cases of domestic violence, he repents by giving his family a honeymoon period in which they can do no wrong; he showers them with gifts and good times. During this period his feelings of inferiority and inadequacy build in response to his feeling out of control. The cycle will be repeated.

X Mr. Smith is a victim of child abuse and is reacting to that, too. He lacks parenting skills. He cannot benefit from examples set by his wife or others because of the rage he feels for his own father's abuse of him. He continues to suffer from that abuse today, and justifies it by abusing others. This is a vivid example of the continuing abuse cycle; it is as if a baton were being passed from one generation to the next.

TOO MUCH, MUCH TOO LATE

Some children grow up strong and secure in their belief of self and their knowledge that a positive relationship exists between them and their parents. Others grow up with feelings of doubt and detachment. We know the parental attitude perceived by a child is the one accepted. In the extreme, children who perceive abuse often grow up to be ultrasensitive to abuse or ultra-abusive.

Where is the fine line between punishment as a negative event, even a vengeful act—Mr. Smith's discipline—and the discipline that builds a child's self-esteem and self-control? Who can say that any of us, when faced with the problems of family life in a complex and stressful society, cannot cross over that fine line between reasonable discipline and punitive and abusive discipline? In this book we shall explore the differences between the beliefs, values, and attitudes that underlie preventive and positive discipline and those that promote child abuse.

When control is severely threatened or completely lost, we may discipline out of anger. While we have come to accept anger as a normal human emotion, we now recognize that anger and its advanced form, rage, can overwhelm the self-control required to turn confrontations into situations where positive behaviors are taught. Far too often, angry discipline is "too much, much too late." This form of discipline is a release for the parent. But it has the devastating effect of teaching children to react out of anger themselves. Or it can teach them to hide feelings, to replace honesty with lying, and replace openness and fairness with a value system that says, "Anything is okay, if you don't get caught."

Not all child abuse is physical; most is emotional: neglect, rejection, avoidance, and failing to recognize good behaviors. Children whose good behaviors are not recognized soon believe they are not good, and often they practice their only other option, bad behavior.

Alberta is a mother of three. She was raised in a home where her mother doted on her. Her mother failed to set realistic limits, and tried to make up for Alberta's rejection and emotional neglect by her father. Her father loved and freely gave emotional support to Alberta's younger sister, Cindy, whom he regarded as intelligent and beautiful. However, he didn't even call Alberta by her name, but instead referred to her as "dumb shit." The interaction between father and daughter was characterized by downgrading Alberta, especially as compared to her younger sister. He would say, "You should be like Cindy; instead you are nothing but a long-legged son of a bitch." None of her behaviors received his approval, neither A's and B's on her report card, nor her musical skills. He could only find fault with her.

As a teenager, she drove to a lake one Sunday afternoon to swim with several friends. Her father found her there and made her walk the ten miles to home, right through the heart of their small midwest town. He drove his car behind her.

At the end of her first marriage, Alberta surrendered her children to her husband. She was then remarried for one year, divorced, and one year later remarried, only to divorce again after three years. She is currently in therapy, living with one man after another in self-imposed isolation from everyone in her family. She considers her life unsuccessful and unfulfilled, having had no positive or meaningful relationships. She continues to seek men who will accept her unconditionally. She then does things that cause them to question her, and when they do, she assumes she is being scorned and rejected.

X Many parents do not *like* to discipline their children. Most teachers list behavioral problems and student discipline as a major area of concern. How, then, does one explain the amount of time spent by parents and teachers disciplining children? I think the answer is that discipline is an outgrowth of our need to control. Power and control themes play a dominant role in why and how we discipline.

Many who reject punishment completely cross another fine line. They treat their children as pals, best friends, or buddies. The relationship of parent and child is lost, as is the responsibility of parenting, including the teaching of essential self-control. Parents with these beliefs often talk about the relative nature of right and wrong. They question how one person can know what is right for another. They frequently add that this is teaching by example. We are all equal. We all have equal decision-making skills. Such an approach is always inconsistent because anything goes. It is shallow and undermines a child's security. Social scientists agree that uncertainty about expected behavior results in feelings of insecurity. Security is found in knowing parental limitations.

On January 24, 1989, Theodore (Ted) Bundy was put to death in the Florida electric chair for murdering more than one hundred young women across this country. He was captured, prosecuted, and sentenced for raping, torturing, and killing a 12-year-old girl. The irony is that this attractive, well-educated, charming man was, in his own words, brought up in a loving home. We do not have all the facts about his childhood, but, whatever the disciplinary practices, they failed him as an adult. Ted Bundy grew up without self-controls and without respect for the fundamental rights of others, the very values that discipline should teach children. He believed that he had the right to impose his will on others, even that he could take their lives.

It is difficult to explain why a family can have one child who is a model person and another who is a monster. Sociologists often observe that equal numbers of criminals, policemen, and clergy come from the same families in similar urban neighborhoods. How does one account for this? Ask any mother. She will tell you that different children are born with different temperaments and widely differing needs for love, privacy, and structure. That is why parents cannot rely on a discipline cookbook. Each child must be responded to differently, but under the same rules for behavior and under the same consequences for infractions. The custom-tailored part of disciplining children is how it is applied.

Should parents be confused about whether or not to discipline their children? The answer is, "No, absolutely not!" Parents have the responsibility to teach their children to respect the existence, beliefs, and rights of others. This respect is achieved only through discipline. Without discipline we become self-serving and self-indulgent. We teach self-discipline to our children by the model we provide of adult behaviors, more than by any words we speak. Children should be given love and security; their parents' restraint of anger in discipline; and their parents' adherence to consistent principles in the presence of understood rules.

Parents teach a vital lesson when they teach kindness, compassion, respect for others, and a sensitivity to what others may bring our lives. They provide a model when they restrain the intensity and extent of their own angry feelings, saying with controlled anger, "That (name the behavior) really makes me angry. I don't want to be angry, because it spoils the good times we have together. So, I expect you to follow the rules we have talked about. I expect you to respect me and my wishes, to show restraint, and to control yourself so that we can enjoy each other."

Children who are treated consistently, fairly, and kindly respond in the same way. Children who are given the gift of life without the parental teaching of respect and restraint fail to learn to respect themselves or others. Lack of respect for self arises from the absence of self-discipline. Its absence shows that teaching did not occur. That may be the fine line between positive discipline and child abuse.

DIFFERENCES
Discipline or Punishment?

A teenager, sixteen years old, recently stood trial for the shooting death of her father. A jury of twelve found her innocent after listening to hours of testimony that described graphically the years of abuse that the girl had endured.

In another case, a twenty-two-year-old man was not so fortunate. He admitted shooting his neighbor eight years earlier with a deer rifle, and described in detail the physical and sexual abuse he had suffered. The neighbor handcuffed and beat him, cut him with a knife on the feet and arms, sodomized him, and burned him on various parts of his body. This torture continued for several years, while the boy, then fourteen, remained silent under the threat of having his throat cut.

The young man's father, an alcoholic, was totally unaware of the malignancy of the relationship, and did not monitor the boy's life. One day the neighbor was found murdered. The crime remained unsolved for over eight years, until the young man was arrested for a minor traffic violation, and fingerprinted. The prints matched those on the weapon used in the unsolved murder years earlier. When confronted, the boy confessed and said it was a relief to have it all in the open. Although the jury believed the boy's story, the law in that state allowed no mercy in cases of premeditated murder. The young man was sentenced to twenty years in jail without parole.

Child abuse and sexual abuse of children are not new. What is new is that more people are talking about child abuse. Times change, and our perceptions of what we will permit or punish evolve, but child abuse and sexual abuse are ever present.

In the case of the young girl who shot her father, the jury sympathisized with the girl's suffering. Other relatives, including her mother, testified that the girl had been beaten terribly for years. The jury accepted the self-defense plea and acquitted her. In the second case, the boy had grown older since committing the crime. Although he was remorseful, he was not sorry. The jury did not find justifiable homicide. The boy will continue a life of hell behind bars until he is forty.

In days gone by, neighbors probably would have lynched the abuser of the fourteen-year-old boy, while the young woman might have been burned at the stake for the heresy of killing a father who had the right to punish her.

CONVENTIONAL WISDOM

Television, radio, and the print media, particularly news-papers, have a powerful influence on our beliefs. So do our friends and other people with whom we exchange ideas or get information. This is called "conventional wisdom."

Conventional wisdom plays a key role in deciding the right or wrong of our parenting practices. Much of what others teach us and the information we use as parents (in other words, how we learn to be parents) gets its approval from a given social order, usually a subculture such as a family or geographic region. In some cultures, for instance, harsh punishment is condoned.

Attitudes of Earlier Times

In the days of the westward migration across this land, families faced strenuous demands. Judged by today's standards, the hardships suffered by children would have caused modern child protective services workers to investigate and to remove them from the care of their parents. Just a little over one hundred years ago it was common for small children to do heavy labor, to sleep on the ground or in wagons during travel, and to sleep several mixed sexes to a bed.

Discipline, like the times, was stern. By today's standards it was harsh. Obedience was a requirement for children. Their lives and well-being, and that of other family members, depended upon their early assumption of responsibility. As late as the 1920s, an eight- or ten-year-old boy might not start school until after Thanksgiving, when the fall harvest was in. He would then leave school for spring planting in late March.

Defining What is Acceptable

Each generation faces the need to reinterpret the social order, one of whose components is child discipline. Each generation must make rules that fit its perceptions of what should be. The result is unstable traditional values. Each generation develops disciplinary practices based on traditional values, interpreted and expressed through conventional wisdom.

Conventional wisdom decides what parental disciplinary practices are accepted by society. But social change, not knowledge nor good sense, is the force that transforms conventional wisdom. Therefore, while certain conventional practices may be acceptable, they do not always have any real value. On the other hand, some highly acceptable practices may have excellent child-rearing values but become outmoded and lost as social perceptions change.

Judeo-Christian Values

Much of the conventional wisdom shaping parental attitudes toward discipline comes from Judeo-Christian teachings. There was a time when the Bible occupied a much more central place in people's lives. The Bible offered a standard for families. Parents understood that their role was to teach respect for others and responsibility for self, to base reason on moral values, and to use principles such as the Ten Commandments as a guide for parenting. People respected these guidelines as great common sense, if not profound wisdom.

This value system has lost much of its impact on modern society. For example, a recent national study found that only thirteen percent of Americans agree with the Ten Commandments and try to obey them. Only nine percent said they never lie.

Problems Change, But Not Values

Fashionable child-rearing practices usually rest on strict adherence to conventional ideas. This is one reason adolescents develop cultures of their own. They resent the adult world's inability to see what they perceive as new problems needing new solutions. They feel that the adult world is merely responding from its tired posture: "This is the way it was always done." The truth lies between these extremes. While the surface complexion of a problem changes, the human values that support it may not have changed.

Issues of Control and Decision Making

Many extreme disciplinary practices do not result from any reasonable approach to child rearing. They are control mechanisms. Recently, for instance, the police arrested a man for tying a belt around his thirteen-year-old daughter's neck and forcing her to crawl down the street, barking like a dog. His reason was that she did not return home on time the night before. He was arrested on charges of child abuse and third-degree assault.

The issue of control begins early in the parent-child relationship. It becomes particularly difficult in the adolescent years, as children struggle to break their allegiance to the home and transfer it to the peer group. The main issues at this time are the values that the adolescents have learned and can now test in the peer group.

Today, adolescents must decide whether to use a controlled substance, such as crack. We consider drug cultures to be new phenomena, beginning in the 1960s and linked primarily to greater affluence in the United States. This is untrue. Many earlier cultures had similar problems, ranging from the Chinese opium dens to common use of cocaine by the upper middle class in Elizabethan Europe and England. A generation ago in America, the substance might have been LSD or marijuana, and before that, alcohol. Although the substance changes, the decision, its consequences, and methods of reasonable parental management do not.

The Limits of Conventional Wisdom

Social perceptions alter, though life's issues remain constant. Conventional wisdom provides continuity in social thought and action by avoiding change until radical reforms appear. Reliance upon conventional wisdom is safe, though often shallow. Conventional wisdom reduces parent-child interaction to a socially acceptable, though superficial, level of communication and interaction.

Conventional wisdom also comes from friends and family, well-wishers who may not be knowledgeable about the history or the characteristics of the people involved. What worked once may not work again. Discipline practices that were effective with one child yesterday may not be suitable with another child today even though the problem remains the same. Conventional wisdom establishes acceptability, but acceptability doesn't make a disciplinary approach effective. It means only that a certain procedure has been used before and can be used again. Conventional wisdom too often looks only to the control technique, and not to what should be taught or learned.

While conventional wisdom implies acceptability, it does not imply a stronger family system. It does not mean that the sought-after value has been learned, tested, incorporated into belief systems, and displayed in children's behaviors.

Value Systems Must Vary

Parenting places an ultimate test on conventional wisdom. Effective parents provide, promote, instill, and even permit children to develop, a workable value structure that fits their personalities. A small-framed, shy boy, who finds it difficult to stand up to others, must be given different guiding principles for personality and social development than large, confident, extroverted siblings or friends. We would not construct the same set of behavioral guidelines and socialization principles for Pee-Wee Herman, Arnold Schwarzenegger, and George Bush. Each deserves a custom-tailored approach. Conventional wisdom does not promote the development of a child's unique and personal value structure. It might be different than the family's.

How are Parental Belief Systems Formed?

Children are born into a world of conflict. Even their own existence may create conflict for parents, especially new parents. In many cases where child abuse is present, parents are single, have limited education and economic means, had poor child-rearing models themselves, and were not ready for parenthood. A premature launch into parenthood reduces the time for mental preparation and building the desire to be a parent.

It is impossible to separate parental belief systems from their disciplinary practices, including punishment. Parental belief systems are a matter of maturity, intelligence, upbringing, information, and social and personal stability. In an actual case, two young parents were indicted for the malicious wounding and neglect of their eight-month-old infant. The parents, themselves undernourished, had been unable to provide food or adequate shelter for their only baby, leaving her in an unheated room to suffer severe hypothermia.

Two Examples of Parental Readiness

Consider the following two examples of how children are brought into the world. In the first, the couple have an education and good jobs. Both have similar family training and developed comparable attitudes toward family and community. They date, discuss their expectations, and prepare for their roles as parents. Their children are born—after months of prenatal planning, diet control, and medical management—into a secure home. The parents wanted these births.

The prospective parents select a name in advance, know the sex of the child, and have a room prepared, possibly monitored for the very breathing of the new child. During preparation, they have discussed child discipline. They are preparing to guide the social learning of this infant, even when it cries. To these parents, the job of parenting means socializing the child. They will teach that life should be honorable and productive, and that the learned social values be acceptable to the larger social order. The child gradually, without any extreme disruptions or discomforts, joins the adult ranks as a contributing member of society.

Contrast the previous scene with another that is steadily growing in our country, the scenario of the illegitimate child born to a mother who is little more than a child herself. According to the National Center for Health Statistics, the number of illegitimate births increased from fifteen percent of the total teen births in 1960 to forty-eight percent in 1984.[1] Over one-half million teenagers, at a mean age of fourteen, give birth out of wedlock each year. Many of their offspring will not be well prepared for adult life.

The transition from adolescence into adulthood is marked by activities that define an evolving maturity, leading to and including graduation, employment, marriage, and parenthood.[2] Deviations from the chronology of these events result in very limited parenting skills.

Many researchers have studied the factors associated with teenage pregnancy.[3] Racial factors, parents without a high school education, and homes with low educational aspirations are among the most consistent identifying variables. Some researcher have found that premarital pregnancy directly relates to a loss or disruption in family roles. Others have named the leading predictors of teen pregnancies as: cohabitation, race, poor grades, high peer activity level, use of illicit drugs other than marijuana, and having dropped out of high school.

Many factors associated with adolescent drug use are predictors of teenage pregnancy.[4] These young parents are less religious, participate more in delinquent activities, have poor relationships with their own parents, involve themselves heavily in peer culture, may be depressed, have low self-esteem, and are prone to risk-taking.

Adolescents may use premarital sex and pregnancy to punish their parents. And it could either reflect a need for security or the need for peer status as an adult.

RICH WORLD/POOR FAMILIES

There is no reason to single out adolescent mothers as the only study in contrasts. Mothers of any age who use drugs (often in combination with other factors) are numerous today. Young women who have married, and then become separated and divorced, struggle with both child rearing and income production. Often, they have little preparation for either.

The effort to obtain the best, in the presence of all that can and does go wrong, is a great paradox within this society. Few past cultures have known the luxuries and satisfactions available in this society. Yet, the presence of misery, ignorance, and social decay challenges us in stark contrast to those values of compassion, equality, respect, and human dignity.

Poverty alone is not a cause of social deterioration. Many families are poor but clean and well cared for, and develop strong positive values. The need for welfare or other assistance is not equivalent to social deterioration, but there is a growing attitude of acceptability of long-term welfare and dependence. Look at the hardships faced by our ancestors in opening and developing this land. Perhaps we have overemphasized our free enterprise economic system to the point of excluding essential human values. Can it be that each successive generation loses some values that guide human interaction, and upon which relationships and understanding are formed? We seem to be slowly giving up the values inherent in the founding of this nation—hard work, self-discipline, and sincere respect for others.

Teaching honorable human values is difficult. Values must be lived and integrated into the human belief system, not as an accessory, but as an integral part of the personality. Children sense insincerity, and they also recognize when something is genuine. So, the values presented to a child must be not only clearly defined and useful for success in life, but also sincerely and genuinely held by significant adults.

THE GOAL OF DISCIPLINE

The first of many purposes of parenting is to provide each new generation with the skills, information, and values that will increase their ability to survive and to give to yet another generation. Discipline is the means by which generations communicate their values to each other. The ultimate goal of disciplining children is to teach the positive values upon which they should base their lives. The goal of discipline is to promote self-discipline.

Effective discipline requires an appreciation of the importance of the skills or behaviors being taught. To the seventeen-year-old recruit, induction into the Marine Corps will be filled with discipline. Much of that discipline is hard to appreciate at the time. Drill instructors have developed a tradition of using self-inflicted punishments, such as physical training, to make their point. It is doubtful that they need the punishment measures such as push-ups or full-gear night runs to do this, but these have a tradition. What is clear is that discipline means obeying authority unequivocally, and that discipline is important in maintaining a military organization to conserve lives and defeat an enemy.

Why is discipline so necessary in the military? Absence of discipline breeds disorganization, and disorganization produces fear. Fear comes from not knowing that one is a part of a larger, organized effort to crush the common enemy. Fear grows when a soldier stands alone, without human support, faced by unknown horribles. Soldiers are human and will have fears; discipline gives them the self-control to overcome those fears. The reward for controlling fears is the support of one's buddies and confidence in one's abilities. The capacity to maintain a rifle in the field is one example of those abilities; being able to strip and reassemble a rifle in the dark conveys a feeling of assurance.

Importance of Social Rules

The military example for learning self-discipline serves as a useful analogy for most social learning. Humans are social animals, and, as such, must learn the rules of the social order. Society without rules would be chaotic.

Children need rules, and the rules must be understood. Teachers have had great success in asking children to develop rules for their classes, and principals are doing the same for schools. I observed a first grade teacher develop the importance of rules by having several discussions about what it would be like if there were no rules. She began by using an example of driving a car without rules. The class found it entertaining, and understood the value of rules and social order. Discipline requires knowledge of the rules, and a consistent, impartial, and fair enforcement. Ideally, those who make the rules establish appropriate punishment simultaneously.

Good Discipline Promotes Positive Attitudes

Parents and teachers will have many opportunities to identify, recognize and praise appropriate behaviors. Parents and teachers who strive to teach through positive discipline never miss an opportunity to praise good behaviors. The belief that children are both good and capable of being good changes attitudes. These attitudes affect everything children believe about themselves. If they believe they are good, their behaviors generally will be good. It is a self-fulfilling prophesy. Children learn values from their own experiences. Approval is a powerful stimulus that furthers learning and motivation.

THE ROLE OF PUNISHMENT AND DISCIPLINE

Punishment, if used at all, should be used to support discipline. In the next chapter, we will look at the main reasons for punishment, one of which is deterrence. There is general agreement that punishment is not an effective deterrent; even capital punishment has had limited effectiveness in deterring crime. What does deter crime? Social learning, which means developing a social conscience, is the only successful deterrent. Social learning is the development of attitudes and behaviors that we can comfortably live by and apply as meaningful social values. The only real reason for discipline is to help us remember that we live in a social order and must protect it.

What is the parent's role in teaching discipline? If the object of discipline is to teach social values, a major responsibility of a parent is teaching children values that comply with the larger social order. Is discipline important in helping children gain control over their feelings while they are learning the rules imposed by the social order? The answer is decidedly "Yes."

Procedural Punishment

The purpose of any punishment technique is to remove or reduce an unwanted behavior. Procedural punishment is the use of negative stimuli in response to the unwanted behavior. A child runs through a room filled with expensive vases; the parent spanks the child for running. A child says a dirty word; the parent denies the child ice cream for a specified time. Punishment should reduce the chances of a behavior occurring again.

The value of this type of punishment depends on the procedure used. The procedure must have negative value strong enough to overcome the desire of the child to behave a certain way. The difficulty with procedural punishment is that not all negative stimuli have the same value. Children who have lived without normal human interaction respond positively, not negatively, to physical punishment such as a spanking. The spanking may not be an aversive stimuli if it provides more contact than the child normally gets for good behaviors. For children who crave parental recognition, human interaction, and peer recognition, even punishment is better than no recognition or continued rejection.

A punishment procedure, even one that has been effective in the past, does not necessarily keep its aversive value. A young child may be punished with a harsh look or a loud voice. As the child develops, the aversive value of the punishment may be lost.

If the expectations for desirable behavior remain constant, and the rules are known (eg., children don't run in the house; children use language appropriate to the social setting), the emphasis should be on how to obtain the desired behavior. Too often the emphasis is on ritualistic punishments that overshadow desired behaviors.

In one family, all infractions of the parents' rules resulted in the same punishment—a spanking with father's belt. The severity and number of blows depended upon the degree to which the infraction was age-inappropriate. There are three boys in this family. They attempted to avoid the "strappings" with the belt, but when it became inevitable the boys dignified the strappings. They depreci-

ated its aversive value by displaying a one-upmanship with each other, a macho response to its use.

As the boys became adults, they shared with their dad how they had learned to insulate themselves psychologically against his punishment. He had observed this but felt trapped into continuing the tradition, as both he and his wife had decided it was the thing to do. Upon probing, the father revealed that his father had used the same punishment. All three boys ritualistically adopted this parental practice with their children, with little change in how they administered it. There was probably little change in how it was received.

Much of a child's socialization requires the suppression or elimination of certain behaviors. We discourage children from such antisocial behaviors as lying, cheating, stealing, and aggression. A punishment should emphasize the social skills a child is to be taught; it should not reflect the mere will or mood of the parent.

Punishment is a tool that generations of parents have used, sometimes reasonably and sometimes unjustly, to modify children's behavior. Punishment can be very effective in stopping unwanted behaviors. It will not teach a new behavior, nor does it build a social or personal value system that teaches what to do and when. Punishment that does not teach values to children is a long-standing, but inappropriate, practice. Punishment for the sake of punishment is rarely effective in obtaining desired learning.

VALUE OF INCREASED ATTENTION

Punishment does obtain the full attention of another. It elevates arousal of the nervous system, increasing the feeling and believing levels of the person receiving it, and on-lookers as well. Boxing is a sport that requires opponents to punish one another physically. Both the boxers and the audience are anxious and alert. On-lookers at a street fight generally become excited.

Parents learn that they may ask a child several times to stop an activity, only to have the request ignored. Once they add punishment to the request, particularly if enhanced by controlled emotion, the undesirable actions change immediately. The proof of this statement can be seen by observing a defiant child who, after receiving punishment, displays no further hostility. When asked if he understands, the response is often an automatic, "I'm sorry," or "I won't do it again."

In elevating arousal, however, there is the risk of stimulating other, equally unacceptable, behaviors. If the child is not remorseful, or feels uncontrolled anger, aggressiveness may result. That is why parents who administer punishment with poor emotional control run the risk of worsening the child's emotional reaction.

Punishment must be provided in the presence of reason, because a purpose for using it is to enhance reason. Punishment must not be administered as an emotional release for the person who is punishing. The old adage, "Punishment is harder on me than you," is true. The parent must struggle to maintain control, using each incident as an opportunity to teach.

The lesson concerns human values and respect for others and their property. That lesson should create awareness that other people must be recognized, and that each of us has an obligation to consider the needs of other human beings. This is why punishment can be a powerful teaching tool, because it creates a heightened state in which the learner receives information. Elevated arousal means that the nervous system is awake.

Punishment suggests that we are asking someone else to learn, to correct, to change in recognition of the principles we are teaching. It is wrong to use punishment as a the force behind this change. Punishment creates a condition where control is removed from one person and placed in the hands of the authority figure, with the prime objective being humiliation. Reason and compassion are in the shadow of this dark force.

ROLE OF PARENTS

Parents assume an initial control that they will eventually and gradually pass on to the children. This control of feeling-driven impulses and recognition of others is an example of being sensitive to reason. Children must learn to differentiate among their needs while developing awareness of the needs of others. Life is not easy; its joys are in the unselfish giving of oneself. The sooner we recognize it, the greater the joy we can experience. A child who grows up without decision-making skills may suffer a serious loss of self-esteem. A child who grows up without self-controls probably will become a victim of self-centered needs.

Teaching Values

People cherish certain ideas or beliefs that we call "values." These ideas express the judgments that people have of the relative worth or importance of things. In America, for example, we characteristically value highly such things as success, beauty, prosperity, and education.[5]

What are human values? Human values are the structure, if not substance, by which we decide ethical and moral issues. Frequently we call them the "ought forces."

Values are personal as well as universal. New lessons in values must continue throughout life. Values are not simply a matter of tastes or perceptions. While values can reflect cultural differences or similarities, they are tied to what each individual respects, supports, and condones—as opposed to rejects.

It is nearly impossible to be consistent and teach basic rules that will apply throughout life without using a solid value system. All children break rules: sometimes to test, sometimes unintentionally because they didn't think, sometimes intentionally to get their way. Broken rules require "fixing"; proper discipline searches for why the rule was broken, and leads to an understanding that it should not happen again. But this is impossible if the family does not have an internal value structure along with the love and consequent forgiveness that separate responsible discipline from destructive punishment.

Teaching Self-Control

Adult behavior generally is not regulated entirely by feelings, whereas children begin life expressing their entire being as emotion. Life begins with two basic feelings: happiness and discomfort. As children grow, they learn to add to, or differentiate between, these two basic feelings. We say that adults display more subtle feelings than children. What we really mean is that adults have a greater range of feelings through which they convey emotions. As children grow and develop, a major parenting objective is to teach those values and skills that prepare children for self-control over their emotions.

An example is the difference in acceptability of a temper tantrum from a three-year-old versus a ten-year-old child. In responding to a three-year-old, the language used, the concreteness of the examples, and the level of understanding reflect the child's maturity. Firmness without punishment would be ideal. The purpose is to teach the importance of social control. Upon command the behaviors should stop. The effort is not to make it physically impossible for a behavior to occur, but to forbid it through teaching appropriate commands.

Following social rules and obeying commands of authority are enforced by rewards and punishments. The purpose of rewarding behaviors is to stress the importance of getting appropriate responses to one's actions. The parents' role is to define social awareness and acceptability. If children are unable to learn appropriate social rules, punishment of unwanted behaviors may be required. Parents' responses to children must be strong and consistent. If not, the values they are trying to teach may seem trivial, or their importance may be viewed as relative to various situations.

Development of Conscience

Almost from birth, children begin to incorporate their parents' values into their developing conscience. Conscience is, therefore, initially defined by the values of the parents. As conscience develops, it incorporates those values consistent with the social order, or it deviates. We base our sense of conscience upon our convictions about what is right; it weakens when children have doubts about the moral principles they have learned.

Conscience, as the seat of values, therefore develops positively in response to those social obligations that involve respect for authority. Conflicts may result when the person's social values disagree with those of authority. Values must be taught consistently and applied to all situations, despite the authority, or conflict also will result.

Values and Social Behavior

Social behaviors, and the differences between positive discipline and abusive punishment, are value-based ideas. The difference in applied discipline between a three- and a ten-year-old child is that a ten-year-old child should recognize commands, if not authority. If he does not, a review of commands that stop unwanted behaviors should be reasoned out at a ten-year-old level, much like the teacher I mentioned earlier. That simple and concrete reasoning should be extended into the child's need to override feelings and to use self-control. Acceptable rewards and punishment should be discussed with the child. The objective is to establish communication and help the child understand the importance of impulse control while learning the values accepted by society.

SUMMARY

Values are the foundation of every social order. These values reside in the teaching of ethical and moral behavior. Therefore, the basis of a culture resides in the communication of each generation to the next. If parents surrender the responsibility for conveying moral and ethical values to their children because it is a tough and demanding role, others will fill the void. If commercial television, for example, becomes the conveyor of moral and ethical values, our society will soon reflect the values of entertainment.

In this chapter, we have considered the social value of punishment. Conventional wisdom, in great part, defines the acceptability of parents' actions, and the prevailing values of society. The primary purpose of punishment is to stop an unwanted behavior. The primary purpose of discipline is to teach values to bring about the development of social skills and respect for the property and rights of others.

A good way to develop children's social learning skills is to use positive discipline to support their learning of values. In distinguishing discipline from punishment, I have described a major role for parents. Parenting is not simply providing information and meeting the emotional and physical needs of children. Such a view is dangerous. Parenting demands teaching respect for others' wishes and desires, which, because they come from an authority figure, are not always acceptable to the child. A child must be taught that he is entitled to his feelings, but expressing those feelings inappropriately is unacceptable. Parenting requires the teaching of decision making and self-control.

TRADITIONS
Origins of a Dangerous Tool

As a boy on my grandfather's farm, I watched young roosters fighting. Usually they fought one-on-one, until one was wounded. Then all the other young cocks would gang up on the downed bird, pecking and clawing until it was dead. I often wondered about the psychology of the gang attack. Years later, I observed incarcerated boys behaving the same way.

My research on punishment has made me marvel at the justifications societies create for their punishment practices. Group punishment of one person is very common, whether society's condemnation of a convicted criminal, a group of children behaving cruelly toward a peer, or members of a social organization, like the workplace scapegoating a colleague. Why do people want to punish others? On a global scale, why do societies seek to destroy other ethnic or racial groups, or even nations, in what might be called a punishment frenzy?

PSYCHOLOGY OF PUNISHMENT

Punishment is humiliating. We talk about punishing the behaviors and not the child. The truth is that the sting of the paddle or any form of reprimand is felt strongly by a child. Who doesn't remember being paddled in school or watching it happen to someone else? First, there is the complete loss of control. Second, there is the urge to fight it. But fighting it always leads to more controls: "Now stand there and take it like a man," or "The more you fight the more you'll get." Usually, the sick sense of humiliation, associated with the loss of control that suddenly floods one's mind, reduces resistance by the simple wish to get it over quickly.

I have heard off-the-record descriptions by high school principals of the best kind of paddle, the best position to stretch the skin, how to inflict the most damage. For many teachers and parents, there is no alternative to corporal punishment. But to rule by only adult control, or to set rules that are enforceable only by corporal punishment, creates fear and an atmosphere lacking reason.

So, the contemporary inclination is to remove the option of corporal punishment. But it can be a powerful tool if used appropriately. I have observed positive changes in children's behavior as a result of corporal punishment. In these cases, the disciplinary process, not the administration of the punishment itself, was the highlight of the experience. A discussion before the punishment gave the youths time to respond to guilt, ponder their behavior, explore alternatives, and actively participate in the punishment process. To be accepted, a punishment must be seen as just and deserved.

On the other hand, I have seen the opposite effect: youths becoming more resistive and rigid in attitude after punishment. For them, the pain of punishment resulted in increased vengeance, not remorse. None of us wishes to surrender to the will of another human being, more so if we are receiving the punishment unjustly. The psychological horrors that accompany punishment can leave lifelong scars.

The psychology of punishment begins with the fact that no one really wants to be punished. If punishment is to have a positive purpose, it concludes with reason, not fear, and it leaves some controls and decision making in the hands of the child.

Punishment and Values

What is the nature of humankind? Are we born in the image of the Almighty, slightly lower than the angels? Or, are we conceived into a world of disorder and chaos, where one person misuses another? Is the struggle of life simply the pitting of one's need to gain control over another, or is there a search for the ultimate good of humankind? If there is an ultimate good, how can it be taught? Does punishment teach the value of good behavior, and does punishment deter willfully wrong actions? Such deep, disturbing questions have caused societies to change, searching for responses that will result in social order with a conscience.

It is difficult to believe that a nation of hard-working, family-oriented people could participate actively or passively in the deaths of six-and-a-half-million innocent people. Bruno Bettelheim's eyewitness account of German behavior toward political prisoners from the late 1930s through World War II expresses what we have learned to date concerning the history of punishment. He writes, "They had no consistent philosophy which would protect their integrity as human beings. . . . They had obeyed the law handed down by the ruling classes, without ever questioning its wisdom. . . . They could not question the wisdom of law and of the police, so they accepted the behavior of the Gestapo as just. The Jewish people were made objects of a persecution, which had to be justified in their (non-Jewish German) minds as being right, since it was carried out by the authorities."[1]

Social psychologists concerned with moral development have tried to explain the difference between punishment as a social control and punishment used to teach human values.[2] The common belief is that morality means conformity to society's norms, but true morality is an internalized standard of behavior. We do seem to use punishment as a way to obtain immediate control, to force others to behave as we believe, often without explanations and without much thought about moral principles to be learned. As a nation, we electrocute, hang, and administer lethal injections to humans who take the lives of other humans. As retribution—perhaps; as a deterrent—possibly. For, while punishment is not an effective deterrent (as I will explain later in this chapter), it is a means by which society communicates moral principles.

The death penalty may sound barbaric, particularly when expressed as the "public's will" in response to murder. Is capital punishment the ultimate control that society requires to protect itself? The death penalty seems absurd when a life sentence without mercy would assure societal protection. Or is it the "public will" to respond in kind, it being logical and reasonable to take the life of one who willfully took the life of another?

This is one thing that critics find so troubling about capital punishment. Are we saying to people who have broken the law that we are teaching them respect for the law? (In the same way, many children receive corporal punishment each year accompanied by the words, "That should teach you a lesson!") Do we honestly believe that punishment is teaching a lesson in human values and reason? If so, how can we believe that the most abusive form of punishment, capital punishment, is itself a deterrent to wrongdoing? Perhaps we punish mightily to convince our children (and ourselves) of the severity of some crimes. The assumption is that punishment must reflect the severity of the act if we are to teach that different behaviors have varying degrees of unsuitability. We scold when fingers get into the cookie jar; we increase the punishment several-fold when the child tells a lie.

Parents and society have an obligation to teach moral values. If an individual is unwilling or incapable of learning these values, then that one must be isolated from society. Our purpose, beginning with the discipline of children, is not to punish, but to teach values that are respectful and appreciative of life, property, and another's beliefs.

What Abuse Teaches

Child abuse is also an act that teaches. It teaches that humans strike out in pain, misery, or anger against a person for whose care and education they are responsible. In each abusive act, parents or teachers show how easy it is to cross the line separating behavior guided by internal human values from the unreasoning and irresponsible behaviors of persons with low impulse control. Actions speak louder than words. Abusive parents refute the morality that each generation carries with it. Morality implies more than a behavioral response to psychological conditioning. Morality involves significant others helping children mature into adults, as they learn to make decisions based on caring and compassionate values. Children think, "If our parents do it, it is probably all right."

THE ANATOMY OF PUNISHMENT

In the last chapter, I distinguished between punishment and discipline. While most systems of discipline include some forms of punishment, punishment has different meanings for different people at different times. A legal definition, first stated in 1867, lists six criteria for an act to be considered legal punishment.[3] Those six criteria are: First, punishment is a privation (evil, painful, devaluating). Second, it is coercive and against the will of the recipient. Third, it is inflicted in the name of the State; therefore "authorized." Fourth, punishment presupposes rules, the violation of which is a formal determination, expressed in a judgment. Fifth, when punishment is inflicted upon an offender, it presupposes a set of values to which both the offender's harmful act and the punishment are ethically relevant. Sixth, the extent or type of punishment is proportional to the gravity of the harmful act, and aggravated or mitigated by the personal motives and temptations of the offender.

As the mood (value sets) of a society changes, so do its views on punishment. Four themes mirror the changing views of the larger society as it wrestles with the concerns aroused by deviant behaviors. Those four basic views are: retribution, deterrence, social defense, and reformation.

Punishment as Retribution

The issue of retribution has persistently nagged the societal conscience of nearly every generation and race of people. Most societies, from the beginning of recorded history, have expounded on the subject. Today, concern for retribution continues in the United States, as evidenced by the seesawing of the various state and federal courts on the issue of capital punishment. Why has humankind had so much difficulty with the idea of extreme forms of punishment for extreme crimes? We can't appreciate the answer to that question until we have walked death row and looked into the eyes of the condemned. Consider the word "condemned." It is cold and hard, hardly a suitable word for a "kinder and gentler" society, one that ostensibly wishes to do well by all its citizens.

In A. C. Ewing's classic book on punishment, *The Morality of Punishment*, the author says that the primary justification for punishment resides in the simple belief that any offense deserves to be punished.[4] There is no expectation of gaining any future advantage by inflicting punishment; punishment is good merely for its own sake.

This idea troubles most of us, but makes perfectly good sense to those who believe in retribution. Advocates of retribution theory assume that individuals choose and act rationally and thus purposefully decide to commit a crime. They argue that the only alternative is to punish that wrongdoing. They believe that for each human act that transgresses a law, a punishment is in order. The punishment should be directed to the offender rather than the social order, even if social conditions may have spawned the offense. Above all, the offender must suffer for a wrongdoing. And the the gravity of the offense should roughly dictate the severity of the imposed sanction.

Retribution and Biblical Teaching. Old Testament teachings further justify society's leanings toward retribution-based punishment.[5] That justification appears to reside in early Jewish law expressed in the Old Testament. The Bible speaks to the need for punishment when crime breeches the peace and renounces the right and responsibility of one person to respect another or his property. Following Cain's murder of his brother Abel, he declares, "I shall be a fugitive and a vagabond in the earth: and it shall come to pass that everyone that findeth me shall slay me."

There is also the relationship between God, the heavenly father, and his earthly children. In Proverbs we find, "Whom the Lord loveth, He correcteth; even as a father the son in whom he delighteth." And in Hebrews there is this reference to God and his children, "If ye endure chastening, God dealt with you as with sons . . . but if ye be without chastisement, whereof all are partakers, then are ye bastards, and not sons."

Punishment for its Own Sake. J. D. Mabbott, a distinguished Oxford Scholar, wrote a justification of retribution theory in 1939, which he continued to revise.[6] He based it on what can be described as a criminal's "just deserts." The argument suggests that society does not have the moral right to make punishment either useful or pleasant. Society cannot give the right to punish; only a criminal act can earn it.

Mabbott's argument represents the view of many today. Those who support retribution will delight in a well-developed example that illustrates his point. Mabbott explains his theory by telling a story of contrasts. He explains the importance of retribution even when it supports a bad law. The principle is that the goodness or badness of a law does not matter, nor does the relativity of the law.

As a disciplinary officer in a college, Mabbott was responsible for meting out punishment for all infractions of college rules. One rule compelled chapel attendance. He agreed that chapel attendance was neither the college's business nor should it be reinforced by a rule. It made no sense to drive boys to chapel through the fear of punishment. Therefore it was not the rule that was important to support; it was the rule breaking that deserved punishment. Mabbott explained, "I certainly did not want to drive others into chapel through fear of penalties. Nor did I think there had been a wrong done which merited retribution. I wished I could have done away with the rule itself as I did not believe that I would have done any differently if I had been a boy myself. My position on the matter was however quite clear. They (the students) had broken a rule; they knew it. Nothing more was necessary to make punishment proper."

There is evidently carryover into today's society from this generation-old theory of retribution. Every behavior that breaks a rule must be punished. The important point is that the punishment is not designed to correct, treat, teach, alter, or redirect a behavior. Punishment is a necessity for all rule breaking. Many people, including parents, believe and practice retribution theory.

A Right to Punish. The justification of punishment theory states that society or its members have the right to punish.[7] Rather than being justifiable on moral grounds, punishment is justifiable because an infraction of a rule exists. There is a transference from the general social belief that justifies criminal punishment to the right of parents to punish.

The most common reason given for retribution is that punishment acts as a deterrent to future misbehavior.

However, as stated earlier, retribution theory is not concerned with punishment as a deterrent. Retribution stands or falls on its own merits, not for any goodness or badness of the behavior that must be punished. The theory maintains that punishment of rule breaking is for the good of the rule, not the rule breaker.

No research evidence supports retribution theory.[8] The data suggest that the only legal or social support of this theory and its practices is the cold hard fact that it is a major factor in the development of our thinking, and we therefore require our justice systems to use it. Beyond its traditional value, it lacks supportable merit. Apparently, we cling to retribution-based punishment because it provides our society a sense of security, of well-being, a sense that we can defend our need for rule making.

Retribution and Child Rearing. Many parents continue to believe that there is an inherent moral lesson, and therefore intrinsic value, in teaching children to realize that punishment follows rule breaking. Some parents who follow this practice recognize that punishment lacks teaching value, but remain unconvinced that it matters. What counts is paying debts; each rule infraction requires compensation.

Traditional child-rearing practices support retribution-based punishment. The reasoning is that society could not exist without rules, and if society has the right to make rules, then so do parents. If society has the right to punish to protect those rules, be they good or bad, then so do parents.

In summary, humankind continues to have a strong need to punish. In support of this, our society has found a theory of retribution that it believes is of value. The principle of that theory is that a social or personal transgression requires the law to impose punishment upon the perpetrator. There is no moral or practical deterrence in retribution theory.

Punishment as Deterrence

Deterrence can be defined as the restraint that fear imposes on those likely to break a rule. Unlike retribution, which supports the punishment of all rule-breaking acts, deterrence relies on the principle of selection. Deterrence has little to do with the act being punished. It looks to the future behaviors of the person committing the undesirable act, and to observers.

The theory is simple: the fear generated by the threat of punishment inhibits others from doing the same and thus protects society. The severity of the punishment is not the question, only that it provide sufficient suffering so that all who might consider the act will also consider the consequences. In this sense, it requires that punishment be administered to protect against such future acts.

On the surface this response appears sensible. It is as simple as "Don't run in the living room, or Mommy will spank." However, where deterrence runs into trouble is in implying that it has carryover, a future promise kept.

The Future Promise Paradox. Deterrence causes much frustration when it is associated with the future promise. If the future promise of deterrent action is to work, it must be practiced consistently. One finds oneself following a strict, by-the-book application of punishments. For instance, the rule that no one runs in the living room is enforced by a spanking. What if a child runs to escape his brother who is about to hit him? Do parents impose the deterrent of spanking? Or, do they regard the child as innocent and face the danger of being inconsistent in their management? Inconsistency could raise the question in the child's mind, "Can I do it and get away with it?"

Yes, it is illogical and wrong to punish the innocent. There are always overriding reasons, and behaviors that are acceptable, even appropriate, given certain situations. There is an obligation to interpret and judge an act against the needs of the person committing it, the people affected by it, and the surrounding circumstances.

Clearly, a child who is taught that killing any human being is wrong may experience difficult emotional and social conflicts when confronted with the military draft. Murder in civilian society is wrong and, under deterrent theory, must be punished. Children may be better off if they understand that some behaviors, given a specific time and situation, have to be adapted. Killing the enemy in a time of war may be condoned, not on moral grounds, but out of society's need to survive.

Similarly, it is wrong to start a fight, and the appropriate social response by the parent is to teach a child how to avoid one. Yet, if a fight cannot be avoided, is it wrong to protect oneself from physical harm? How thin is that line? Only as thin as societal values concerning punishment are relative.

Punishment then must fit the crime. At times the degree of punishment is simply not severe enough to prevent certain behaviors. In my town, for instance, a parking violation is two dollars if paid in twenty-four hours. The parking garage at my office costs three dollars. On rainy days, it is worth the risk of the two-dollar fine to have across-the-street convenience and avoid the price of the parking garage. It is hardly worth the price of public outrage and the loss of confidence in a justice system to suggest, say, flogging a person for overtime parking. Still, overtime parking violations might decrease if the penalty was raised from two to five dollars.

Arguments Against Deterrent-Based Punishment. The most persuasive argument against deterrent-based punishment is that it seems ineffective. Punishment does not appear to deter unwanted behaviors in small children, nor does criminal punishment appear to keep adults from committing crimes.

A second argument asks why, given that each of us is capable of heinous crimes, the general population rarely commits these crimes. The answer is that punishment does act as a deterrent for *most reasoning people*, thus preventing many crimes that would otherwise be committed. Have you ever been angry enough to destroy another person's property, or possibly even take his or her life? What prohibited that thought from materializing into conscious awareness, even to directed action? Could it have been the memory you had of the hard spankings your father gave you when you imposed your will unreasonably on someone else? Could it be that subconsciously you relate that to the long trial, death in the electric chair, and all the humiliation and financial hardships this would bring to your family?

The Value of Association. Some argue these factors are real and do hold the line for those who function in the realm of conscious reason. But not all people do just that. There are those who seemingly have no concern for the consequences of an act. For those persons, the thoughts accompanying the idea of punishment are in themselves not reformative.[9] Children seem to remember and associate all the unhappiness connected with punishment.

They tell us that those associations played a larger role than the actual punishment itself.

I have observed principals eloquently using this idea of associating punishment. They have children recount their misbehavior repeatedly, picking out the parts where they sensed the consequences and saw their mistakes stand out as if in slow motion. Once each act was blown into a bigger-than-life portrait, the next line of discussion was to look at alternatives; then at why rules exist; and then a self-incrimination period in response to the repeated question, "Why did you do it?"

Finally, there is the matter of establishing an appropriate punishment. Expert principals handle this elaborate process with, "You tell me the options and you tell me the punishment you deserve." While children wait, shivering and uncomfortable, in the presence of warmth and genuine concern, they must judge their acts and pass sentence. They must relive their decision and now see that there were alternatives, while judging that act and themselves. Does it work? Yes, it has a strong deterrent value. Children generally set harsher and more devastating punishment than adults would. When the principal reduces the sentence, it suggests that truth and a clean conscience are worth the price of the punishment. And, it is the rare, very angry or forgetful child who repeats the act.

The Value of the Deterrent. Research on the effectiveness of punishment as a deterrent to crimes has not been overwhelmingly positive. An important issue is the value of the deterrent. The difficulty with society setting the value on a deterrent is that some may consider the risk of some punishment worth the cost of being caught (e.g., my earlier example of the parking fine in my town). The relative value of punishment is influenced by several things. For example, the possibility of being sent to the principal's office may present such imaginary horribles to a school-age child that this threat has a much greater deterrent value than the death penalty may have for an adult. Then again, few adolescent or adult perpetrators believe that they will ever be apprehended.

Most children do not try to draw unfavorable attention to themselves. But some children receive so little attention, either negative or positive, that they do not differentiate between the two. Their craving to be noticed overwhelms reason, and a trip to the principal's office carries with it all types of peer and adult recognition. Besides, the office is an interesting place. The office is a wonderful busy place in stark contrast to the drab bore of the classroom where the best sport is to hear Jimmy, who cannot read well, stumble. The entertainment and public recognition at the office may be well worth whatever happens.

Also, the value of the deterrent resides within the authority of one administering it. How many mothers locate the deterrent factor of punishment when they say, "I will tell your father"? Perhaps the source of the discipline has more to do with its power as a deterrent than the type and amount of the discipline. There are schools where policies prohibit teachers from administering corporal and other forms of punishment. The authority lies with the principal; therefore, his name or presence has a deterrent value.

But what is the power of the deterrent in having a student go to the office for rule breaking and, once he arrives at the office, find that the principal has stepped into the hall? Too often what occurs within the office is ineffective adult monotone accusations that merely promote argument. Such experiences create adversarial relationships, not the self-examination that should be the essence of punishment.

After years of watching both pros and neophytes handle such problems, I sense the value of discipline lies in the communication that surrounds it. When discipline is reduced to merely an action and reaction, and the only value in the reaction is punishment, little is gained. Without self-examination, the only result may be a poor attitude in children who view themselves as only the problem, rather than part of the solution.

Thus, the use of punishment can have preventive value. But a very important distinction must be made between how punishment acquires meaning for children and the meaning adults assign to deterrents. Adults who have committed a criminal act frequently ignore alternatives, even when they possess the reasoning to know what to do.

Learning Selflessness. Children must be taught to be thoughtful of the feelings and rights of others. Unfortunately, today's society has become extremely self-serving and hedonistic. Self-fulfillment and self-aggrandizement are in vogue. Children are bombarded with multiple examples of this viewpoint, such as: "Get it while you can"; "Take care of number one"; "You are the most important person"; "Take good care of yourself." Selfishness is taught and, in many respects, is very natural. Selflessness is less easily taught. That lesson, beginning with the recognition of others and ending with the Golden Rule, is terribly important to both the individual and our society.

Once selflessness is learned, the child considers others when making decisions, and considers consequences more carefully. These children will grow to adulthood seeing the value of not getting into trouble. They are not dependent on the hollow values of the belief, "I won't get caught because I am too smart." Instead, they will attempt to draw upon values that address and recognize others.

Factors in Effective Punishment. Punishment does not deter other rule infractions and displays of unwanted behavior unless it also teaches people how to behave and why. Punishment without teaching simply promotes an aversive response toward the larger society and authority figures. The best example of this is when someone, such as a parent or principal, imposes himself as the punisher and a person to be feared. A punishment system lacking the elements of self-examination and behavioral alternatives merely teaches children to respond negatively to conflict. Their negative response will be to test the external authority continuously. The ultimate goal is to achieve internal impulse control and self-control, not to maintain the constant presence of punishment as an external deterrent. To be effective, punishment must acknowledge:

- the differences between types of offenses;
- the differences in people, the reasoning that promoted a behavior, or the absence of reasoning;
- the differences between social groups in the larger society;
- the conflicts between group norms within any family, school, or small social order; and
- that when a model exists there must be consistency between what it practices and what it preaches.

Punishment as Social Defense

Many educators, sociologists, and psychologists agree that parents discipline children to acquaint them with the rules for future independent functioning. Adulthood is defined, not merely as the end of puberty, but as entry into independent decision making.

Our society attaches its very survival to the decision-making skills of its members. This requires that people learn social rules early and maintain a conscious awareness of their importance. It is under those conditions that such ideas as "the greatest good for the greatest number" become pillars upon which our social order rests. That belief has been tested repeatedly, and thus far it appears that the thread that holds the social fabric together is those values we teach to our youth.

A few short years ago many parents were horrified to see their children wear their hair long, grow beards, and extol the virtues of marijuana and LSD while protesting governmental policy through open rebellion. Many wondered: Has American society lost a sense of its direction? Or is there something wrong with the war in Vietnam? Today most of us agree that it was a little of both, but we proudly proclaim that the democratic process withstood this test. Perhaps there was a huge sigh of relief as we watched the hippie generation give way to the current yuppie generation in pursuit of vertical mobility. How interesting that several former hard-core social reformers are now seated in state and federal congresses! The truth is, they are probably raising more hell than they ever did, but now within the framework of governmental processes.

Historically, our nation has viewed punishment as necessary for teaching conformity to social rules by all citizens, be they children, new immigrants, or criminals. Many consider punishment as a cornerstone of the American way of life. It acts to protect society and repress crime. That historic view has now been modified; the current theme promotes punishment as a teaching tool explicitly designed to prevent social wrongdoing. For the criminal it is a reeducation technique, consisting of treatment, therapy, and rehabilitation. Society continues to claim punishment as necessary, but now in a more positive light. The positive use of punishment is brought clearly into focus with the parents and the home serving as center stage in the teaching arena.

There is also growing awareness that society is not always right. Social moral values are relative to a particular time and a specific situation. Therefore social defense and its techniques, including punishment, must be considered as part of a political philosophy. Recent world events, for example the violations of human rights in South Africa, Haiti, and Iraq have increased our sensitivity to the idea that the state can be just as wrong as the person. Justification of an action because it does the greatest good for the greatest number is no longer acceptable.

Punishment, when understood as an instrument of social defense, must be viewed entirely differently from its use as retribution for past wrongdoing, or as a deterrent against future wrongdoing. Social defense goes much further by suggesting that punishment is a device to protect both the society *and its individual citizens*. No longer can a child be punished only on the basis that a rule has been broken.

First, it must be determined that the infringement was a *conscious and deliberate* effort to break the rule. Second, the antecedents and existing conditions must be considered and allowed for as important contributors. Third, it must be guaranteed that the child knew the rules and could interpret them correctly given the situation in which he found himself. Fourth, any punishment must be provided in the context of the human values that it represents. It is not to be administered out of duty, or some inherent right of the punisher to set and enforce rules. Punishment must make sense and be understood as a dimension in the human social order. This lesson begins at birth and continues to death. Finally, there must be a recognition that human behavior is imperfect and that it occurs in an imperfect world, under socially relative policies.

WHAT VALUE IS PUNISHMENT?

It is a simple fact that not all unwanted behaviors can be prevented. Not all punishment is effective in deterring future unwanted behaviors, even when harsh corporal punishment is used, or when the threat is capital punishment. Not all punishment is effective in helping the child learn the social values we feel are desirable.

There is also the possibility that punishment required by the child as an attention-getting device has little long-term value in the ultimate reform of thoughtless and unwanted behaviors. Reformation is a two-way street involving both society and the individual. The greater our individual freedom, the greater the likelihood people will use these personal freedoms to impose their will on others. Without freedom of speech, there would be no communication of personal values, but those values and their communication may also threaten another's rights. Often we speak of a utopia where ineffective and unsatisfactory forms of punishment will be unnecessary. Until then, some means of stopping unwanted behaviors must be used. Until there is no need for punishment, parenting requires it.

It is my sincere wish that punishment be seen as a set of procedures (techniques) for teaching human values by which our society can improve with each generation. However, during the last four thousand years of written history there has been no major upswing in "right over wrong" in any culture, any nation, anywhere on planet earth. People and the problems they face today seem much the same as in previous generations. One reason for this consistency is that societies have generally clung to the traditional approaches in hopes that reformation would occur for the succeeding generation. I therefore question the effectiveness of most forms of punishment, *unless the techniques used convey the learning of new behaviors*. Love and positive direction teaches more than punitive punishment.

We look to the value of history to avoid the careless repetition of mistakes. We have learned that inappropriate punishment may result in increased violence. We have learned that harsh punishment results in the resentment of authority. We have learned that punishment for the sake of punishment is folly, and without redeeming value. We have learned that without values and moral instruction, punishment provides only authoritarian control. We have learned that punishment without compassion, absent respect for the values and feelings of others, has the cumulative effect of damaging human decency. Punishment communicates a distorted view of human problems and the message that force is an acceptable quick fix to unwanted, undesirable behavior. It is a limited solution and, as a quick fix applied universally to any wrongdoing, it lacks the individual recognition and custom-tailored response to shape desired behaviors.

The question remains, what value is punishment? The answer must be in the behavioral principles being taught, in the values to be learned. We want children to learn to obey rules, acquire self-discipline and impulse control while developing an appreciation for life, respect for self, and responsibility toward others. Without self-control there is no morality. Without the values implied in the laws of morality there is no social order. Humans are social beings differentiated from the lower animals in behavioral response forms expressed as higher order values. What then is the basis by which caring for others, social responsibilities, and values that require control over an imperfect human nature, can be taught as an expression of self-serving interests?

Punishment is a strong form of communication. It is a message and it speaks a message. Before you punish, ask why. Search for the reason, the value, the purpose. Control of situations and control of people is sometimes necessary, but it should be recognized that the lesson to be taught is not simply control.

In brief, punishment is a dangerous tool. It is no better or worse than the purposes for which it is used. It can be a powerful communication and teaching technique through which values and the most desirable human conditions can be obtained. Or, it can be like a hammer used to treat all human failings and human problems as though they were nails. Punishment for its own sake is ineffective and profits society very little. It may even beget more and harsher forms of punishment, until it becomes self-perpetuating and brutal.

SUMMARY

Parents and teachers have been supported historically by the laws of the land in administering punishment, unless the punishment was cruel and unusual. The intent of the law was to encourage discipline and to provide support for heads of households. With caring parents, a philosophy of just punishment was rarely abused. To those seeking an extra measure of control, an acceptable philosophy of punishment became a moral right to dominate others.

Today, there is an effort to alter traditional disciplinary practices. Punishment, as a means of teaching obedience to rules (laws), and the common traditional practices of corporal punishment have been called into question simply in terms of their long-term effectiveness. In some states, corporal punishment has been banned from the schools by law.

In the recent past we have seen the reemergence of a family orientation in our society. The learning environment and the desired outcome for children's behavior is resuming a more important and central place in the home. The adult "me" focus has begun to give in to a greater joy in the stability of the home and the ability to give to others. While it is difficult to measure precisely this trend—or predict its longer-term effect—it is clearly positive.

Why do some parents cling so tenaciously to poor practices in the face of new knowledge of their ineffectiveness? Perhaps old practices die hard because they embrace some of the human elements that we might wish were not so prevalent. Among those are the need for control in contrast to reason—the need to obtain blind obedience as opposed to a value-motivated response. And then there is always the issue of time. Physical and verbal controls are not labor intensive responses. Physical and verbal punishments require little parenting skill. Physical and verbal punishments obtain a quick response . . . at first.

ABUSE AND NEGLECT
A Tragedy of Generations

A fourteen-year-old boy intentionally knocked a computer from its stand in his school classroom. School officials called in the parents for a conference concerning their son's behavior. At the meeting, the father immediately vowed to whip the boy and, in fact, did shove his son during the interview. The boy was suspended from the school for a week. On his return, he had bruises on his face and arms and layers of welts on his back. The father had "disciplined" his son.

There is a war; one that started with the dawning of the human form on this planet. In this war the battleground is the human heart. The opposing forces are love as a great kindness in which we are free to give of ourselves, and a word called love which some use to control others.

All parents should love their children; they should happily change their dirty diapers, clean up after them, and forgive them when they break things of value. Frequently, the parents must live without, so that their children may have. Love is selflessness, but not all people are able to be selfless. Children do not get to choose their parents.

Not all people of child-bearing age are emotionally equipped to rear children. Many men believe that the father's role in parenting is to "make babies." After that, children "get on their nerves"; many wives have been violently abused for "having those kids."

Child abuse is an accident waiting to happen. Rarely do parents plan child abuse. It is a response to putting our own needs first. Also, the fears and the incompleteness we experienced as children spawn a cycle. That cycle is not necessarily someone's fault; it is a collective tragedy of generations. Children are born into a harsh world where life is not always considered valuable, and responsibilities are too frequently thrust upon those who are unable to meet them.

Every day the headlines underscore accounts of the abuse and neglect of children. When human services workers or school officials need to take action, they consider the degree and intent of the abuse. Tragically, all cases do not end with the children living "happily ever after." Too often, if these children survive childhood at all, they live emotionally scarred lives, repeating the abuse of their childhood on others.

IS CHILD ABUSE NEW?

Child abuse is as old as recorded time. For centuries children were considered property, and, as such, their parents were completely responsible for their treatment. There was a time in America when parents were thought to be doing their duty when they chastised a child abusively. The Society for the Prevention of Cruelty to Animals far predates any child protective group. There is probably no more abuse today than in the past. But we view child abuse differently now, and report more to authorities than ever before.

Immediately after World War II a pediatric radiologist wrote about broken bones with unspecified causes.[1] He attributed these "accidents" to parental irresponsibility. By 1962 C. Henry Kempe used the term "battered child syndrome" to describe fractures that lacked adequate explanation, and therefore must be parent-inflicted.[2] Because this medical diagnosis addressed the parent's role, it allowed that medical providers could predict and prevent child abuse. There were two major flaws in this viewpoint. First, it is difficult to predict child abuse based on physical evidence alone. Second, it is difficult to suggest treatment based on the physical data obtained from battered children without social and psychological information.

By the early seventies, researchers had begun sociological research into physical abuse.[3] Much of their work did not include emotional abuse or neglect. They focussed on the incidence, prevalence, and social determinants of physical violence to children. The culmination of the efforts of many people brought federal legislation in 1974 when, on January 31st, President Gerald Ford signed Public Law 93-247, the *Child Abuse Prevention and Treatment Act*. By 1977, most states had responded with regulations that required reporting and protective child service investigations. The states continued to use legal definitions addressing "harm" to the child, including in the language a wide array of mistreatment, neglect, maltreatment, and abuses. The abuse of children falls principally into two groups: physical abuse and emotional neglect.

LEGAL DEFINITIONS OF ABUSE AND NEGLECT

The following definitions are used in the *Child Abuse Prevention and Treatment Act of 1974*:

> An abused or neglected child is one whose physical or mental health or welfare is harmed or threatened with harm by the acts or omissions of the child's parents or other persons responsible for the child's welfare. "Threatened harm" means a substantial risk of harm. "A person responsible for a child's welfare" includes the child's parent, guardian, foster parent, an employee of a public or private residential home, institution or agency, or other person responsible for the child's welfare.

"Harm" to a child's health or welfare can occur when the parent or other person responsible for the child's welfare:

> Inflicts or allows to be inflicted upon the child, physical or mental injury, including injuries sustained as a result of excessive corporal punishment. "Physical injury" means death, disfigurement, or the impairment of any bodily organ. "Mental injury" means an injury to the intellectual or psychological capacity of a child as evidenced by an observable and substantial impairment in the child's ability to function within a normal range of performance and behavior, with due regard to the child's culture; or

> Commits or allows to be committed against the child, a sexual offense, as defined by state law; or

Fails to supply the child with adequate food, clothing, shelter, education (as defined by state law), or health care, though financially able to do so through their own means or through offered financial assistance; for the purpose of this Act, "adequate health care" includes any medical or nonmedical health care permitted or authorized under state law; or

Abandons the child, as defined by state law; or

Fails to provide the child with adequate care, supervision, or guardianship by specific acts or omissions of a similarly serious nature requiring the intervention of the child protective service or a court.

Child abuse laws are found in:

- *Criminal Law* - state statutes that identify child abuse and neglect acts that are criminally punishable.
- *Juvenile Law* - state statutes that authorize the juvenile court and human service agencies to provide protective services and, when necessary, remove the child from the home (parents).
- *Reporting Acts* - require reporting of suspected child abuse and neglect that cause sufficient concern to require an investigation of the home by the appropriate agency of the state.

Generally, the laws provide these protections to age eighteen, but in the cases of handicapped children the laws may be extended to age twenty-one. Each state has its own definition, but most states include the following elements:

- *Physical abuse* - nonaccidental injury, which may include severe beatings, burns, strangulation, or human bites.
- *Neglect* - the failure to provide a child with the necessities of life: food, clothing, shelter, proper supervision, or medical care.
- *Emotional abuse* - placing unreasonable demands on a child to perform above his or her capabilities, and doing so in an excessive or aggressive manner. Examples include constant teasing, belittling verbal attacks, and a lack of love, support, or guidance.

The Importance of Intent

There are many factors in the determination of child abuse. First, child abuse frequently requires the presence of "intent." A parent must deliberately cause physical or emotional damage for a disciplinary practice to be considered abusive. Accidents, or actions by parents that can include injury but were unintentional, usually will not be considered abusive. In short, child abuse requires evidence that the intention was to cause injury.

INCIDENCE OF CHILD ABUSE

The American Humane Association reported that over 1.7 million cases of child abuse came to the attention of authorities in 1984.[4] Most cases included neglect with minor physical injuries, with about ten percent of the reported cases involving psychological maltreatment and mental cruelty.

Psychological maltreatment does not receive the attention, nor is it as clearly defined, understood, or proven as physical abuse. It is rare to see a report of psychological abuse alone. When one appears, it is difficult to prove in the courts. The meaning of psychological abuse varies across the states.

Psychological maltreatment is a denial of the child's development of self-esteem and interpersonal skills by unreasonable acts that punish (not physically). It involves acts of rejection, inappropriate control, extreme inconsistency, and deliberately subjecting a child to traumatic experiences by alternating patterns of repeated overstimulation and emotional deprivation. Refusing to provide help for an emotionally disturbed child also may be a form of psychological maltreatment.[5]

This year, parents will kick, bite, burn, or punch three out of one hundred children, to extremes and with great regularity.[6] When child abuse occurs with sufficient physical force and sufficient regularity, fatalities do occur. Eight out of one hundred children will experience unusual and extreme punishment at least once before their sixteenth birthday.

In 1981, an analysis of case records in eastern Pennsylvania found repeated maltreatment reported in sixty-six percent of the cases.[7] In thirteen percent of the cases, the incidents were not validated. Among the validated cases, seventy-nine percent showed evidence of physical abuse. Emotional abuse was second at thirteen percent, and sexual abuse followed at eight percent. There was overlap among the three, given the high percent of repeated incidence. Gross neglect was a primary overlapping condition and was present in twenty-five percent of the cases, and especially present where mothers were under twenty years of age.

FORMS OF ABUSE

A family was reported to the Department of Human Services for allegedly abusing their eighteen-month-old son. The child's aunt filed the report. The human services worker made the investigation and found the family to be safe.

Headlines later reported that in a fit of rage because the child had dirtied his diaper, the father used the child as a human plunger. He broke his child's neck by repeatedly jamming him head-first into the commode.

Physical abuse of children includes any nonaccidental physical injury caused by a child's care giver. It may include burning, beating, branding, and punching. By definition, the injury is not an accident. But neither is it necessarily the intent of the child's caretaker to injure the child. Physical abuse may result from excessive discipline, or from punishment inappropriate to the child's age or condition.

Maltreatment of children takes a variety of forms. Most service providers and researchers list nine categories:

1. Physical abuse
2. Sexual abuse
3. Physical neglect
4. Medical neglect
5. Emotional abuse
6. Emotional neglect
7. Educational neglect
8. Abandonment
9. Multiple maltreatment

Physical Abuse

It is impossible to list all the symptoms or forms in which physical abuse appears. One very significant evidence of physical abuse is an unusual bruise or laceration, one that is not normally seen on the body of a child of a specific age. Infants with breaks in the upper arm are an example. Cigarette burns on the buttocks or feet, rope burns on the neck or torso, and injuries to the genitalia are other examples. Obviously, not every rope burn on the neck is a result of child abuse. Abuse is generally practiced with great regularity.

Some parents intimidate their children by using cruel and unusual punishments. If they always have a cigarette and the child is difficult to control, they may substitute the cigarette for a more appropriate form of punishment as the very presence of the cigarette may induce desired behaviors. Generally, we can classify physical indicators under the following headings:

Unexplained bruises and welts:

- on the face, lips, and mouth
- in various stages of healing (bruises of different colors, for example, or old and new scars together)
- clustered, forming regular patterns, or shaped like the article used to inflict them (electrical cord or belt buckle)
- on several different surface areas (suggesting the child has been hit from different directions)
- regularly noted fading (old bruises or marks) apparent when the child returns to school after an absence, weekend, or vacation

Unexplained burns:

- cigar or cigarette burns, especially on the soles of the feet, palms of the hands, back or buttocks
- immersion or "wet" burns, including glove or sock-like burns and doughnut-shaped burns on the buttocks or genitalia
- rope burns on the arms, legs, neck, or torso

Unexplained fractures:

- of the skull, nose, or facial structure
- in various stages of healing (showing they occurred at different times)
- multiple or spiral fractures
- swollen or tender limbs
- any fracture in a child under the age of two

Unexplained lacerations and abrasions:

- to the mouth, lips, gums, or eyes
- to the external genitalia
- on the backs of the arms, legs, or torso

Unexplained abdominal injuries:

- swelling of the abdomen
- localized tenderness
- constant vomiting

Human bite marks:

- especially on young children, reflecting recurrent or repeated use, and adult in size

The most common physical evidence includes:

- An imprint on the skin from an object such as a clothes hanger, belt, belt buckle, electric cord, hand print, or teeth marks
- An injury that curves around the body because it was made by a belt, hose, or rope
- Injuries that are centralized on the face and head
- Bruises of various colors, suggesting that the injuries occurred over time
- Abrasions that are in various stages of healing, pointing toward continuing injury
- Injuries on a wide area of the body, indicating repeated blows from different angles and directions
- Repeated burns from hot liquid poured or thrown, glove-like burns inflicted from immersion, or object shaped burns from cigarettes, cooking utensils, pokers, etcetera

Emotional Abuse

A nine-year-old boy repeatedly fails every subject. His parents request an interview with his teachers. At the interview, the mother consistently points out that the boy is adopted and that his older sister, who is their biological child, does very well academically. On subsequent testing, teachers from this interview find that the boy never finishes his tests. He works so slowly and methodically, fearing a wrong answer, that he only manages forty percent of the work demanded. He lacks self-esteem. The parents reject him as stupid.

As maltreatment of children leaves the physical realm, it becomes more difficult to investigate and detect. In the broadest sense, emotional abuse means actions by parents that slow down or interfere with the healthy personal and social development of the child.

As the states attempted to define mental injury, wide variations occurred in their interpretations of the federal law. There was a prevailing fear that they could not find the means to investigate mental injury fairly and responsively. Nevada developed a statute defining these behaviors: "a substantial injury to the intellectual or psychological capacity of a child as evidenced by an observable and substantial impairment of his ability to function within his normal range of performance or behavior."[8]

Two states avoided verbal entanglements in guidelines by delegating authority to child protective agencies to investigate and respond to referrals alleging emotional abuse. Virginia and Mississippi refer to harm to emotional, intellectual, and psychological functioning. The agency guidelines in these states stipulate that there must be a connection between the parent's or caretaker's behavior and the child's mental problems for mental abuse to have occurred. This behavior must either cause mental difficulties or perpetuate them in some manner. The behaviors of the caretaker may be obvious, subtle, explicit, stated, or implied.

Some examples of caretakers' behavior or threat of behavior taken from these two state guidelines are: behavior that is rejecting, intimidating, humiliating, ridiculing, chaotic, bizarre, violent, hostile, or excessively guilt-producing. Mississippi also includes scapegoating of one child in a family and custody struggles where children become pawns and witness their parents belittling, harassing, or blaming each other.

"It Begins in the Ear"

The emotional interaction between parent and child reflects the personalities of both. Parents have the authority. They also set the expectations for children's behaviors. Not all parents love their children, nor offer it to them unconditionally. Many set unrealistically high expectations for their children's achievement and behavior. Many parents are rigid in how children will fulfill these parental goals. Unrealistic pressures to do well in school, athletics, drama, or music create tremendous anxieties for children. Children who do not measure up or fail to meet these expectancies soon believe they are unable to succeed, that they are worthless, and therefore failures. These beliefs generalize from academic achievement to social skills; they affect all activities. Children become forlorn and unmotivated; they do not believe in themselves, and without self-esteem, they soon live up——or down——to the prophecies they make for themselves. As they mature, they frequently are anxious, despondent, and depressed, viewing themselves as lost causes in a hopeless world.

Other parents control their children through fear. They communicate these fears to their children so strongly that the children believe them. Children who are convinced that the world is full of frightening elements quickly become rigid and fearful, unable to enjoy things or people for fear that having fun will cause calamity.

There are parents so wrapped up in themselves and their needs that they do not have time for their children. Often this would appear to be simple emotional neglect. But it is not simple, and it frequently causes children to believe that their parents neither want nor love them. Children growing up in this environment often strive to earn their parents' recognition, feeling only emptiness when they succeed. They have little warmth or emotion to give, and live their lives beyond the bonds of loving and caring relationships.

Some children are taught that they are bad. The most common instance of this is the single parent who refers to the child as "no good, just like his father (or mother)." In other cases, children hear that they are going to grow up to be "bad," just like a relative who is in jail. At the extreme, parents may tell a child that he or she is good, and loved, but display actions that suggest the opposite.[9] A major theory of juvenile delinquency is that it begins in the ear. Children who hear that they are bad, and that they constantly need punishment, frequently manifest just those behaviors.

NEGLECT

Neglect seldom stands alone. Neglect accompanies physical and emotional abuse and may be viewed as an aspect of these other patterns.

Each year reports mount of children locked in rooms or closets. Isolation is both physical and emotional abuse. Not all isolation is physical removal. There are families where the parents live in silence; no one speaks a word at the dinner table, and there is no interaction at all within the family. Laughter is rare, and children have no exposure to parental emotions and self-control of those emotions. Children learn to define acceptable degrees of emotionality and emotional control by modeling parents and in interaction with parents. If that interaction fails to occur, children may be frightened by their emotional responses and afraid to display them. When they do display them, they may be out of control.

Behaviors in children that may be caused by injurious mental or emotional stress are: an excessive need for sucking, feeding and sleeping problems, unrealistic fears, bed-wetting, stuttering, lethargy, depression, runaway behavior, stubborn or defiant activity, poor school performance, poor peer relationships, extensive denial, suicide threats, property destruction, and violence toward others.

Physical Neglect

A three-year-old girl fell down the stairs while her mother was talking on the phone. The child refused to stop crying. After checking the child for cuts, the mother decided that the child was crying just to get attention. The mother put the girl on the couch and told her to go to sleep. The child had suffered a concussion in her fall. She lapsed into a coma and died shortly afterward. No charges were filed.

A grandmother had to care for her daughter's unwanted child. The grandmother worked shift work at a local factory. She took the child to the job site and left her in the car while she went to work. The child suffocated in the car that the grandmother had locked tightly for her protection. Charges of neglect are pending against the grandmother.

The main difference between neglect and abuse is that neglect, unlike abuse, may be unintended. Neglect may be more a failure to provide—an omission rather than a purposeful action. Abandonment is the most extreme form of neglect, nevertheless, parents abandon thousands of children each year. Parents leave children at doorsteps, in gas station rest rooms, or other public buildings. Extremely neglected children receive attention and care from local and state governments under these provisions.

Many states have updated their child neglect statutes. Previous legislation, which guided juvenile court activities, provided for neglected and delinquent children. Twenty-five years ago, many county governments offered homes or farms both to the elderly who were unable to provide for themselves and to children classified as dependent. These children were frequently abandoned or came from homes where parents were unable to care for them due to physical or mental illness.

Educational Neglect

The mother of a fifteen-year-old girl stood trial this year for educational neglect. The girl had missed a total of fifty-four days of school attendance, with the approval of the mother. The school system referred the case to the Department of Human Services which decided to prosecute when the mother refused to force her daughter to attend school. The mother received a jail sentence, but the daughter, who within a month of the trial turned sixteen, formally dropped out of school. The presiding judge placed the family under court order to oversee the girl's attendance either in school until she is eighteen or until she has successfully completed a GED program. The mother will appeal.

Some parents fail to see the value of education or, in another sense of the word, either do not respect the larger society which requires public education or are afraid of interacting with school officials. In these cases, children often are truant from school, and school authorities seek the investigative power of the courts and protective child service providers.

Educational neglect may stem from the inability of parents to provide. Parents who are unable to provide clothing or feel they or their children cannot gain social acceptance may attempt to avoid humiliation by not sending their children to school. In other cases, the intellectual levels of the parents are low, or living conditions make travel in inclement weather impossible. Families who have escaped to a simpler social setting, often far from main roads in remote rural settings, or those remaining anonymous in inner-city slums, find school attendance a social or physical stress.

When the water supply freezes, or the car won't start, or the house lacks heat, the family may remain in bed. Survival becomes more taxing and more compelling than concern for regular school attendance. Problems associated with dropping out of school and irregular attendance often become clouded in an atmosphere of ceaseless and unmanageable family difficulties. So, school attendance becomes an important factor in child neglect. To suggest, however, that all educational neglect is simply a matter of social/physical issues would be incorrect. School attendance is one very large factor in identifying children from families who cannot cope with stress.

Irregular school attendance is a clear symptom of abuse or neglect. It should not be treated as the child's problem, but rather as a family problem. Schools that manage educational neglect as a parent- or child-generated condition and deal with it by expulsion and exclusion only enlarge and inflame the issues. Many poor families find little assistance or compassion for their problems and feel all social forces massed against them. Such dissonance only exaggerates the social sensitivity of those presenting symptoms. Truancy often suggests that a child or a family system is in trouble and needs help. It makes no sense to punish a child for truancy for reasons beyond either his or his parents' control.

Legal Status of Emotional Neglect

It is difficult to separate emotional injury and emotional neglect.[10] The causes may be similar, and the children's observed behaviors also may be similar. Many states refer only to mental injury in their neglect or abuse laws. Others use the word "harm," in any of its forms, and their laws are ambiguous and open, if not silent on the subject. Some states are more specific about the kinds of injury apparent in emotionally abused and neglected children.

THE PROBLEM OF PARENTING

The question is not whether parents cross the line from reasonable discipline to abusive punishment; they do. The question is what is their intent. Discipline designed to obtain growth and development is a healthy and required responsibility of parents. Not every parent does it perfectly. We all fall victim to undesirable actions.

Few parents know what to expect from parenting and how to manage it. Some parents are playing out a role in a generational cycle of abuse; others are warring with personal demons such as drugs, alcohol, and their own personal adjustment difficulties. Not all marriages are perfect, and some are dangerous for one or both members. Some parents are violent, and grew up responding to violence. Some lose control and some never learned control; others find passive means of punishing their children through personal, social, physical, and emotional neglect.

Physical or emotional abuse currently occurs in approximately one out of every thirty homes in this country. Emotional abuse is difficult to confirm. Conservative estimates place it in ten to thirteen percent of the cases reporting physical abuse.[11] Many of us believe (and there is a growing body of data to support the belief) that emotional abuse is more devastating than physical abuse over the long term. Evidence also suggests that emotional abuse may be occurring at an alarming rate, and at socioeconomic levels where families would never consider physical abuse.

SUMMARY

No summary can adequately describe the devastation, the pain, and the continuation of child abuse cycles across the generations. Clearly, greater awareness leading to active and successful prevention and intervention must develop, and soon.

SEXUAL ABUSE
A Toxic Relationship

Recently, in West Virginia, a thirty-nine-year-old man was charged with four counts of sexual abuse against a former neighbor. An eight-year-old girl testified that the neighbor molested her in his bedroom after she brought him a light bulb one evening. "He told me not to tell anybody 'cause he told me he would get in trouble," she said. She said he stopped when her mother came to his house looking for her. The mother called the police after finding the girl without her undergarments.

In a similar case, two young girls aged seven and nine were allegedly sexually abused by their thirty-one-year-old male baby-sitter. After suffering silently, the girls finally told a counselor at school. The baby-sitter stood trial for eleven counts of assault and sexual abuse and was found guilty. To protect the integrity of the girls, the court allowed them to testify shielded by a large blackboard. That way they would not have to look at the man who had hurt them. The convicted rapist appealed on the grounds that he had been prevented from facing his accusers. The appeals court overturned his conviction.

Most authorities believe that more than fifty-six percent of incidents of sexual abuse occur in the home with family members. Since the issues of this book concern parent-child relationships, the use of discipline and punishment, the teaching of values, and the setting of moral standards, this discussion will concentrate on sexual abuse within the family structure.

GROWING AWARENESS

Sexual abuse makes good copy for the news media. It sparks public interest because it represents a major moral indignity. To the average American it is the most revolting form of child abuse. Sexual abuse is parenting at its worst.

As both the reporting systems and the professions who use these data become more sophisticated, the number of reported cases of child sexual abuse is steadily increasing. Sexual abuse is probably not growing disproportionately to any other social or psychological problem confronting our society today. What is occurring is that we, as a society, are becoming more sensitive and aware of its existence.

Our society is far more willing to address this issue today than it was just ten years ago. I can remember when it was unheard-of. This was not because it did not happen, nor because it was not believed, but because of lack of awareness. Main Street America simply could not deal with the sexual abuse of children. This is the defense mechanism of denial, a psychological condition that affects groups as well as individuals. For years we denied the existence of sexual abuse, and in so doing we have denied relief to the victims and treatment to the abusers. Denial is a massive lie, a great cover-up.

We are now willing to talk about sexual abuse in the news media, and face it when it happens to someone else, but much about it remains locked deeply away in parents' and children's minds. The truth is that there are too many victims, of past and present offenses, many of whom will carry their secret to the grave. Our present understanding of child sexual abuse is primitive. But, as the level of awareness grows, so will information. Today sexual abuse is a social concern that challenges every social and moral belief system, and every value that our society upholds. Now it is simply too apparent to ignore.

INCIDENCE

Approximately eight percent of children in America are victims of sexual abuse.[1] Although one usually thinks of child sexual abuse victims as female, at least three percent of American males also have been victims of child sexual abuse. A classic work establishes that nine to forty-five percent of adult American females, and three to nine percent of adult American males, were childhood victims of sexual abuse.[2]

Why such a wide range in the estimates? The problem lies in the hesitancy of individuals, including those who understand the social and psychological impact of sexual abuse, to admit it and bring it into the open. Disclosing sexual abuse is especially difficult for men. Having been sexually abused is a threat to masculinity; denial is much easier than recognition. Evidence is growing that the incidence of sexual abuse in males is much higher than currently believed and reported.

In a study based on self-reported data, ten percent of the adults said that they had experienced sexual misuse before age sixteen.[3] Nineteen percent of college women in the New England states were victims of abusive sexual attacks before the age of seventeen. Another study reported that up to sixty-two percent of women have had either noncontact or physical contact sexual abuse by age eighteen.

From 1982 to 1985, a total of 1,059 children, from three months to sixteen years of age, was seen at a large city hospital with the chief complaint, sexual abuse.[4] Nine hundred and forty (eighty-eight percent) were female, and 119 were male victims. Sixty-nine percent were whites, twenty-eight percent were blacks, and two-and-a-half percent, Latins. The mean age of the victims was 8.3 years. The males' mean age was 7.4 and the females' was 8.4 years.

Each year, it appears that the nature of the reported direct sexual contact becomes more intense.[5] Some studies found that forty-six percent of the cases reported were classified as indecent exposure. Indecent liberties in most studies account for about thirty-nine percent of the cases. These are noncontact types of sexual abuse. Although they may not carry the full ramifications of direct physical encounters, even noncontact sexual abuse has a severe impact on a child. Victims report forcible rape in six percent of direct contact cases, with intercourse resulting in three percent of the rape cases. There is evidence that anal and vaginal intercourse are increasing each year in rape cases.

Again, we may now be more willing to ask if intercourse has occurred and to believe that it has. Evidence suggests that education of children and increased public awareness has resulted in a greater realization that incest and sibling sex happen. A few years ago educators emphasized teaching children to avoid strangers who might try to get them into their cars. No longer do we educate children only about the "stranger dangers." We now ask them to be aware of the "bad touches and bad secrets."

"Incest" and "rape" are two of the most attention-getting words in the English language. Both words signal a transgression of the line between respect for another's status as a child, and an adult's individual desires. In child sexual abuse, these two words are frequently the same. Rape usually occurs as the perpetrator's expression of the stifled need to overcome, to dominate, to be powerful, to feel powerful. It is clearly a product of poor impulse control and may be associated with gang presence, anger toward a family member, drug or alcohol use, social isolation, or extreme social rejection.

PROBLEMS OF DEFINITION

There are no clear guidelines for a broadly applicable definition of sexual abuse, mostly because it has been a deeply hidden social problem. Sexual abuse is not easily discussed or described, especially by victims. Further, violations may not result in immediate consequences: often the effects do not emerge for years.

Incest is the sexual exploitation of a minor child by a parent, parental figure, grandparent, stepparent, boy- or girlfriend of the parent, older sibling, or any other person who has a custodial or guardian relationship to that child. This type of relationship implies responsibility for the child in the family, neighborhood, or community.

Clinical records from the State of Texas show that of 112 reported cases of child sexual abuse occurring over a one-year period, 103 were parent-child, or otherwise incestuous.1 Of the incest cases, five were father-son, two were mother-son, and the remaining cases were against daughters. Father-son and mother-son incest are rarely reported. Incest with daughters is much more common.

The predominate incestuous patterns are those of father-daughter, stepfather-daughter, and maternal boyfriend-daughter. Older research literature suggested that incest most frequently occurred as the daughter entered puberty, usually around age twelve. More recent data suggest that it begins earlier, when the child is ten or slightly younger. It starts with sexual familiarity; bathing together, showering together, sleeping together, being alone together for long periods when the mother is not home. Much of the early initial contact is fondling. One study found a full thirty-three percent of the female children who became victims of sexual abuse engaged in sexual play activities with adults before age six.[6]

A question of resilience of the human system comes into play as well when we try to define sexual abuse. Is there such a thing as minor sexual abuse? Are there normal sexual interactions that occur between minors as either incidental play or sexual curiosity? When do innocent sexual innuendoes take on serious sexual implications, especially between minors and adults? The extent of damage cannot be gauged only in the type, severity, or frequency of the abuse. Sometimes the constant threat of sexual abuse is extremely damaging to the victim.

WHEN DOES IT BEGIN AND END?

The age range for the onset of sexual abuse varies widely, from six months to twenty years.[7] Most happens to children between eight and twelve years old. Again, part of the difficulty in research statistics is the reluctance of victims to report their abuse.

The age range at which abuse ends is from three to thirty-one years, according to documented cases. The age of most frequent abuse is twelve years. While we know much about the onset and even duration of incestuous relationships, there is little information concerning why and how they end. Most researchers believe that short incestuous relationships end because one of the participants becomes fearful. Whether evident or secret, incestuous relationships cause both social and personal stigma. Later we will review the aftereffects of the termination of incest.

According to several studies, the duration of an incestuous relationship may be from less than a year up to twenty-four years. The average duration is an imprecise figure. For most boys, termination occurs at puberty. It appears that by this age boys have sufficient physical strength to resist the sexual aggressor. This is not the case with girls, particularly those who begin such a relationship at puberty. There is limited evidence to say that if father-daughter and stepfather-daughter incest begins in early puberty, it may continue as a longer-term love relationship. It may become a passionate interaction in which the incestuous relationship challenges and even replaces the marital one. One conclusion is that the shorter the duration of the incestuous relationship, generally less than one year, the less likely it is that there will be intercourse. This finding appears in about fifty-five percent of the cases reported.[8]

Most studies agree that the so-called fixated molesters (fixated with male or female sexual and psychosexual development) lose interest as the child becomes sexually mature. For some molesters the act takes on the characteristics of incest as the child becomes adult in both development and appearance. For instance, a grandfather perpetrator, who began with his granddaughter at age five and remained active with her for several years, did not lose interest until she began to lose her childlike features. Victims with childlike characteristics do not threaten these adults sexually; but as the child approaches adulthood, and begins to develop physically, these molesters cease. They feel threatened by maturing sexuality because it begins to approximate a relationship with an adult sex partner, perhaps one with whom they have had poor or strained relationships.

No longer should we believe that molestation occurs at puberty or later. We now know, based on recent careful research, that sexual abuse may begin well before puberty. Studies from both the United States and England agree that fondling generally begins in the six- to eight-year-old age range.[9] However, it is often not reported until years later. There is a significant difference between the age that the molestation begins and when it is first reported. Younger female children tend to be afraid; they don't know what they should report, or don't know how to report abuse. Reporting occurs when girls are older, understand the significance of the act, and experience it as a serious obstacle to their sexual and personality development.

When children are under age twelve, males receive more physical and sexual abuse than females. The reverse occurs after age twelve. Women do more abusing of male children under age twelve. After male children attain age twelve, other males become the primary abusers. What makes age twelve the turning point?[10] It appears that before age twelve, little boys are more irritating to their exhausted mothers, who then cross the threshold of their frustration tolerance, and physical and sexual abuse occurs. Near the age of sexual maturity, girls become the target of sexual exploitation for male members of their families and for male nonrelatives. At any age, male incest victims are more often victimized by males than by females.

PROVING SEXUAL ABUSE

Sexual abuse may involve fondling, masturbating, being required to masturbate others, and forced oral or anal intercourse. Intercourse includes direct contact plus penetration. Sexual abuse also can include becoming the subject of sexual exploitation such as child pornography.

Proving sexual abuse can be difficult. It requires more than just a reported history. Legal and social investigations are important, but a physical examination is essential. Positive findings generally include evidence of trauma to the perineum, vulva, or rectum. Evidence of trauma to the vulva includes fresh tears, scars, or a widely enlarged vagina. A positive test for acid phosphates or the microscopic presence of semen also confirms sexual abuse. In reviewing studies where there is a complaint of sexual abuse, generally about forty-one percent of the cases include evidence of penetration.[11]

Other physical contact occurs in about forty-two percent of the cases where physical evidence of penetration is not evident. These acts include fellatio, cunnilingus, masturbation of the adult by the child, and fondling of the child by the adult. Indecent exposure occurs very rarely by itself. Vaginal intercourse occurs rarely in children under the age of six, with less than five percent of girls under this age reporting it. Anal intercourse, for both males and females of all ages, occurred in about one third of the cases of confirmed physical contact.[12]

Venereal Disease

Positive diagnosis of venereal diseases is present in one and one-half percent of sexually abused children. Gonorrhea is present in about half the cases. Chlamydia occurs in about one quarter of the cases, primarily adolescent females with more than one partner. Syphilis is present in only about one percent of the cases. Very few children have venereal herpes.[13]

Emotional Effects

Emotional mistreatment in parent- or adult-child relationships is not so easily proven. In a widely publicized sexual abuse case, a well-known plastic surgeon went to jail for refusing to produce her daughter for unsupervised visits with the child's father. She insisted that the father had sexually abused the child. The father, also a doctor, has maintained his innocence throughout the ordeal. Nevertheless, the mother vowed to remain behind bars until the child reached the age of eighteen. Since this meant the child would spend at least six years in hiding, the seriousness of the concern is evident. The mother refused to allow the father even supervised visits despite court rulings to allow this.

Psychological or relationship misuse may cause more damage than direct physical contact. Sexual humiliation compromises the development of values, moral principles, and healthy relationships with same-sex parents or members of the opposite sex. The proof, however, is elusive.

DIFFERENCES BETWEEN BOY AND GIRL VICTIMS

There are striking differences between boy and girl victimization. Boys are more often sexually victimized by someone other than their parents, and more likely to have come from poorer families and broken homes. Boys suffer more severe physical abuse than girls. The mother perpetrators are generally poorer, under greater home stresses, and more frequently combine physical and sexual abuse. Young male victims, contrary to popular belief, are more frequently abused by stepfathers than are girls. They also tend to come from larger families and to live with their natural mothers.

The Home is Not the Safest Place

Boys tend to come from families where sexual abuse is widespread throughout the family. Male children receive more forceful abuse, and are abused more frequently, and by a wider range of family members. They are, more often than girls, forced to engage in more sexual contact, and contact of a wider variation, such as masturbation and oral sex, than are girls.[14] Unfortunately, male children are less likely to be believed, and therefore less likely to be removed from the home and to be seen in counseling. The sad truth is that eighty percent of sexual abuse cases involve a parent or guardian. The home is not the safest place; as one local policeman put it, "more children are sexually assaulted by their baby-sitters than by a rapist off the street."

The percentage of teenage girls who experience sexual abuse at home and then become prematurely sexually active within their peer group is high. An important note is that this group consists of younger adolescents, who tend to mature early. Their early physical maturity appears to create undisciplined sexuality. The degree of promiscuity among these twelve- to sixteen-year-old girls results in the highest out-of-wedlock pregnancy rate among adolescents. This age group experiences more sexual disease. They also seem to have more socially related problems within peer groups, academic problems, discipline problems both at school and home, and substance abuse.[15]

BLAMING THE VICTIM

Parenting involves providing children with information and protecting their sexual interests and beliefs. Sexual exploration and interests are a normal part of growing up. What child didn't want to catch some glimpse of his parents in the nude? What child didn't experience the curiosity of their own developing sexuality and want to learn more? I remember as a boy when an older man in my community convinced me that masturbation led to physical weakness, baldness and deformities such as cerebral palsy. There was also a time I believed that sexual intercourse could, in itself, cause syphilis and blindness. I remember reading a paper on venereal disease brought back by a new military recruit during the Korean War. After reading it, I became deathly ill.

There remains today probably more misinformation surrounding sexual beliefs, resulting in sexual taboos, than any other area. It is astonishing how much misinformation is frequently, purposefully, given out to preadolescent and early adolescent boys to obtain a shock reaction.

One theory proposes that children are sexually aggressive and exhibit provocative sexual behavior toward adults.

There is little research support for this theory, however. Children are generally loving and trusting, believing in adults. They frequently attempt to accommodate adults on the adult's terms and under conditions established by adults. One adult, sexually abused as a child, related her experiences: "I played doctor a few times with the neighbor boy, but that was a far cry from the sexual acts that I was asked to perform on my stepfather." Children are coaxed by flattering attention. They are ordered by adult authority to do unfamiliar things—actions so far beyond the scope of anything they would have thought about on their own that they do not know how to act. Therefore they comply.

Oedipal Interests

Freudian psychiatry, with its emphasis on the interrelationship between mental development and psychosexual stages, has spawned many theories that research studies do not support. Among those is that children, as they begin developing feelings of attachment to the opposite-sex parent, become rivals with the same-sex parent for their father's or mother's love. Based on Greek mythology and the story of Oedipus's love for his mother and rivalry for his father, the psychoanalyst believed his client had incestuous tendencies. Even if a child does sexually desire the opposite-sex parent, the required self-control falls to the parent. There may be some examples of children abusing their parents sexually, although, upon initial search, I have been unable to find case reports.

Parent rape, or incest forced by the child, rarely occurs. I am sure that if it does occur, its basis is neither love nor attraction. I believe (and the data on rape support this) that rape is most frequently driven by hate, more than lust or uncontrolled passion, and never love. The point is, even if all things are possible and some are true, parents have an obligation to teach self-control. They do that by modeling self-control and moral principles.

I remember a father whose fifteen-year-old daughter I saw on the complaint that she was still speaking baby talk. When I observed them in clinic, she wore a dress that was much too short, little cotton socks and black strapped patent leather shoes like three-year-olds wear. In the waiting room she sat on her father's lap, and he caressed her and talked baby talk to her. In examination, I suggested that she need not use baby talk to me. She stopped immediately. The inarticulate speech characterized by a mild lisp ceased and she spoke perfectly. Upon returning to the waiting room, however, she resumed the baby talk. Clearly, she acted immature to please her father, and he richly rewarded her for retaining those infantile behaviors.

Incest takes many forms. A common one is to reward and thereby condition children to display certain sexual behaviors that meet parental expectations. This belief makes more sense than believing that all prepubescent boys covet their mothers sexually, and daughters, their fathers. Explanations that deny parental responsibility and decision making, that justify irrational and irresponsible behaviors of parents, are mere simplifications and useless.

SEXUAL EXPLOITATION

Child Pornography

By the late 1970s, there were 264 monthly pornography magazines in America depicting the molestation of children. Films about the sexual abuse of children earn multimillion-dollar profits. Child pornography is a big and serious business.

Studies of children involved in pornography reveal that they have experienced serious psychological harm from such abuse.[16] Anxious and depressive behaviors are common, with themes of denial and anger directed at the adults who should have protected them. These children tend to be withdrawn, avoiding social contact and demanding secrecy. Because they fall outside normal social structures, they are prone to antisocial behavior.

Child Prostitution

There is an element in society that cannot adjust to normal sexual acts with mature adults. Many adult perpetrators may be responding to childhood-related sexual experiences; many are simply experiencing limited psychological adjustments. The illegal and degrading nature of child prostitution makes investigation difficult. It is hard to figure out the incidence or even the lower ages to which childhood prostitution extends.

Children from the streets, many runaways, some kidnapped, and some lured by money and secrecy, work for short or long periods as prostitutes. The psychological effects on small children who do not comprehend the consequences of such acts are enormous. Older children understand what they are doing but feel either out of control or under the control of others. This has the psychological effect of limiting personal adjustment so that many will be antisocial, unable to develop emotional relationships, or unable to live well-adjusted adult lives.

A BURDEN OF MALE VICTIMS

Female children represent most of the victims of childhood sexual abuse.[17] The result is that they receive the most attention. Female victims have received so much attention that we live with the danger of automatically associating sexual abuse only with girls, forgetting that boys face this hazard also, and in very different ways. It is simply difficult for many in our society to imagine the sexual abuse of males, therefore a layer of misunderstanding and mistrust grows up around it.

Imagine a group of young adults telling the story of significant events in their lives and how those events have affected them. A young woman describes her childhood abuse, either by members of her family or strangers. This comes across as totally believable and it is understandable in a profound psychological sense by the group.

Let's change the scenario. Standing in front of you now is a two-hundred-pound weight-lifter who is currently earning $100,000 per year as an insurance executive. He begins to describe how sexual abuse during childhood has affected him. It seems unreal and unbelievable. Young men understand this reaction and so have remained silent over the years. They have been afraid to come forward or even admit the abuse to themselves. They assume the general reaction of society would be critical and call their masculinity into question. For many men, being helpless or passive any time in their lives is equated with homosexuality, which is repulsive to them. The result is that sexually abused men suffer in silence, victimizing themselves.

If all abused persons could open up to tell their stories, seeking support and understanding (including self-understanding), fully half the consequences associated with this problem would disappear in the next generation. Until that time, as one young man put it, "I am ashamed to talk about it, and even if I did, who would believe it?" Such disbelief constructs a dark psychological closet, with an opaque door, guarded by precious male ideas of invulnerable masculinity.

Incidence of Male Child Sexual Abuse

A well-known study of college students revealed that nearly twice as many girls—nineteen percent as opposed to nine percent of boys—had experienced sexual abuse from adults.[18] A major difference is that the female victims reported that their childhood sexual experiences with adults had been primarily with family members. That finding is not shared with the men. Only seventeen percent of the males had been victimized by members of their families. There is some general agreement that most sexual perpetrators are men who were themselves abused as children.[19]

Current reports estimate twelve to fifteen percent of rape victims to be males.[20] It is now also believed that older boys are more often victims than are reported. Abusers of male victims frequently subject them to fellatio or sodomy. While physical injuries are uncommon, the experience is very threatening psychologically, as it is a complete loss of control with accompanying intimidation. Contrary to public opinion, offenders are heterosexual at least as often as they are homosexual.

Most confirmed pedophiles, who abuse many children outside the family, prefer young males.[21] Boys who are sexually abused internalize the trauma, because of the humiliation of having "failed" to live up to society's expectations regarding masculinity. They react through self-destructive activities resulting in such characteristics as obesity, anorexia, self-mutilation, suicidal responses, over-medication, or depression. Some boys completely externalize the trauma through acts of child abuse, spouse abuse, or murder.

REACTIONS OF BOYS VERSUS GIRLS

Girls tend to internalize trauma and often react self-destructively. Other symptoms of female victims include: hyperactivity, excitability, recurring fears, nightmares, and crying spells. They may act out in the home and in the community through defiance, delinquent acts, and drug and alcohol abuse. Boys become angry and confused. A high percentage blame themselves, seeing themselves as incapable of controlling the acts that precluded their ability to see themselves as responsible for their lives. Unfortunately, most victims feel responsible for what happened to them. One common long-term effect, experienced especially by male victims, relates to psychosexual confusion and an identity crisis. Some boys fear homosexuality or become homosexuals.[22]

Following is an example of this confused development.

A young man was sexually molested for six months when he was ten years old. The offender was a twenty-eight-year-old man the boy had met while swimming. The sexually abused boy did not report the molestation. Years later in counseling he reported suffering from chronic depression, poor self-image, and a persistent fear of homosexuality. He said that he felt a strong need to prove and assert his manhood.

When he graduated from high school, this man married an unattractive, dominant woman ten years older than he and the mother of a six-year-old daughter. He probably chose this woman because she was a strong, motherly type who would direct most of his behavior. The daughter provided him a nonsexually threatening sibling relationship. During the early years of this dependent relationship, he expressed himself through an exaggerated sexual relationship with his wife, seeking sexual activities five or six times each day. He performed quickly and denied his partner sexual gratification. If she acted as the aggressor or assumed a dominant role, he immediately became impotent.

After two years she became pregnant and refused his sexual advances, further threatening his manhood. He responded to this perceived rejection by molesting his stepdaughter. He now could assert his manhood without fear of threat.

This infantile reaction, following from his molestation at age ten, shows his inability to seek a normal adult male-female relationship. Instead, he had strong needs to be dependent, as long as it did not question his sexuality. When his wife, who functioned as a mother to his dependent needs, rejected him, he moved his sexual exploitation to a nonthreatening person, a little girl. He directed his molestation to combat real feelings of homosexuality.

Boys who frequently experience pleasure, if not a thrill, during molestation, and identify with their abuser, become active rather than passive participants. They often become homosexual later in life. Homosexuality is a justifying response to the loss of control, if not the psychological surrender and enjoyment provided by the childhood sexual

act with another male. Thirty-six percent of male prostitutes had been molested as children.

Women who were sexually abused as children also have
adjustment problems, stemming from lack of trust, that
affect intimacy in adult life. Some of these victims have
multiple marriages, some become lesbians, and others
suffer from various forms of sexual dysfunction.[23]

Female victims may become promiscuous. This confirms their belief that men are only interested in them as
sexual objects, and that it is their only real value in a
relationship. They are often pleased by the attention men
pay them, but limit the relationship to an overinvolvement
in sexual activity. This shallow relationship allows other
areas of the relationship to deteriorate. Although pleasur-
able at first, there is frequently an abusive quality to the
sexual aspect of the relationship. This quality overflows
into all areas of their relationship and life, inhibiting
personal growth and fulfillment.

Other women victims react by failing to develop sexual
interests. They frequently are dominating and try to
assume control of most situations. Maintaining control
during sexual relations results in limited relationships with
men, and they frequently seek men they can dominate.
Another avenue is for female sexual victims to relate to
men as father figures. They often select men who will
resent the forced role, but who do not have the strength
to combat it. The response of these men will be to work
themselves to an emotional edge where they become
alcoholic and then abusive, playing into the destructiveness
of the relationship and often becoming victims of domestic
violence. Women faced with such perceptions have low
self-esteem. Often, the unresolved issues reappear several
times throughout their adult lives. It takes very little

additional stress to produce severe psychological disorientation or psychosis.

Parenting is often a difficult task for adult women who were molested as children. Because their emotional development was thwarted, especially in the need for trust in the caregiver and emotional nurturing, they feel jealous of attention directed toward their children. Many resort to substance abuse as a tension reducer, often falling to alcoholism. Others become overweight, or act in ways that repel others; this reaps a self-fulfilling consequence of lowering further their already low self-esteem. Over seventy percent of prostitutes interviewed have histories of childhood molestation.

RIGHTING THE WRONG

One researcher has developed an intervention model that includes not only the social and psychological aspects but also offender-victim motivations.[24] The four components of this theory are 1) emotional congruence—or the will, desire, and reason to abuse a child; 2) sexual arousal; 3) sexual gratification; and 4) blockage of normal sexual arousal and gratification. The abuser must meet his or her emotional needs through sexually abusing children. Emotional arousal through mature sexual expression with consenting adults is somehow blocked.

The first and farthest-reaching component of any treatment program is involvement of the entire family. Frequently, it even involves the extended family or significant others who contribute to the family system by providing emotional strength and support, or models for child rearing or disciplinary practices.

Prevention

Prevention remains the most desired form of intervention. Most of the preventive educational programs on child sexual abuse have been for children. That may not be prevention at its root cause, only a minor side step. Active intervention with children restores emotional awareness, and features self-control, emphasizing that children have the right to control access to their bodies. Belief in one's own judgment is important, because most children lack confidence about knowing whom to trust; the result is that they do not trust anyone. If they cannot trust their judgment, then they may not know whom to let touch them, or whom to touch, and where.

The issue of trust also arises in knowing who can help, and when to get help. Films developed for children such as *Penelope Mouse*, about a mouse whose uncle sexually abuses her, leave children with the view that only mice become abused. Even "good-touch, bad-touch" programs bring out unreasonable fears. Children see them as good information for "other kids." Most children believe, "It will never happen to me."

Treatment

If preventive efforts are in their infancy, treatment is not yet born. To date, treatment of adult offenders trails society's major concern for punishment. Rehabilitation of sexual offenders has become a treatment program in many prisons, but the current design of prisons is to incarcerate, not rehabilitate.

Interventions find it difficult to address the long-term carryovers into adulthood resulting from child and adolescent abuse. Besides distrust, victims frequently feel helpless and out of control, forever in the control of others.

There are sexual offenders who are on a pathological search for expression of sexual frustration. They continue justification rituals that create unbroken cycles of sexual abuse, as the attractiveness of children and their lack of threat overwhelms rational thought.

Treatment is slow, and can only begin when a person is psychologically ready. Long-term behaviors are prevalent: being unable to relate in a complete and mature relationship, being unable to perform sexually with adults, and seeking violence or desiring abuse. Sexual abusers tend to beget sexual abusers, that we know. They also tend to be lonely, depressed, and anxious, with poor psychosocial and psychosexual adjustment. They are fearful, and have incomplete relationships with their children, as if they were afraid they might be attracted to them. Or, they may sense the depth of their abuse and resent it more because it happened.

Abusers often have interrupted relationships with their parents and suffer from high divorce rates and many marriages. They are prone to eating disorders, substance abuse, and alcoholism. All this requires treatment, but these are only symptoms of a deeper confusion resulting from limits on their psychological growth as children.

They are angry and frequently hate. Whom do they hate? Their parents, the people who are kind to them, who do for them; their families. Why? Because love is threatening and may put them into a role relationship where others would see them as a hollow shell, unable to show mature levels of caring, compassion, and giving.

LINGERING EFFECTS

Research data is conclusive: sexual abuse of a child seriously affects psychological development and the ability to grow into mature, confident adulthood. Childhood sexual abuse spawns more abuse in the next generation in such forms as domestic violence, poor partnering, and poor parenting.

Sexual abuse creates a psychological scar. It creates abuse cycles; it creates dependency on substances and faulty relationships; it destroys psychological independence and maturity. It makes life extraordinarily difficult for its victims, most of whom did not go in search of it, and wish it had never happened.

The cycle of misuse passes from one generation to the next. Sexual misuse creates imaginary, and sometimes real, parades of horribles for children; feelings of guilt, fear, shame, and remorse. These lead to despondency, depression, hopelessness, despair, and even violence.

Sexual familiarity in one generation may result in sexual misery in the next. Human sexuality is an important psychological area in the development of children. Abnormal development of sexuality, through control measures such as fear or misinformation (as "masturbation will make you blind"), or through verbal abuse, marks several generations to come. Sexual development is a trusted area of parent responsibility that requires careful management, thoughtful modeling, and a value structure based on respect and responsibility.

What Should We Teach Children?

Should we teach children rigid rules on sex? The answer is a resounding "No!" Initiation of sexual abuse is generally not within the child's control. Developing additional rules for the child to follow may be seen as only another pressure, easily misunderstood and generating needless fears.

Should children be dealt with freely in a laissez-faire environment where anything goes? The answer to that question is again definitely, "No." Children require structure and information, and that information should be appropriate to their current stage of life, so they can understand it.

What we adults say to children is less important than what we do, particularly regarding sexual abuse. Actions have a powerful daily influence on children's moral development; they instill the values children will grow to accept and live by.

SUMMARY

Accounts of sexual abuse provoke strong emotional reactions. Sexual abuse threatens the very soul of what we think humankind can become. It threatens the bonds of trust between adults and children. Children require protection and care. They must have an opportunity to learn appropriate behaviors in an atmosphere of security and emotional support. They must have an opportunity to develop values that will serve them as adults. If they grow to adulthood under the threat of abuse—where security and trust is lost—they may spend a lifetime justifying that betrayal. We now understand that child abuse often begins a destructive self-sustaining cycle. To justify and affirm the abuse we have received, we abuse those who place their trust in us.

Sexual abuse may be the epitome of all that can go wrong in a society. Now that it is out of the closet, let's go beyond the punishment in which we wish to enshroud the perpetrators. Instead of fine-tuning the penalties for sexual abuse we should probe the moral, social, and psychopathological features of this disease as we would a serious plague . . . a cancer of the soul.

WHY?
The Origins of Child Abuse

A fifteen-month-old child was brought to the emergency room of the University Hospital at the request of neighbors, following twenty-four hours of a high fever and several convulsions. The mother revealed that the child had previously received treatment for fractures of the right femur (thigh) and an infected scalp wound. These allegedly resulted from falling from a tricycle.

On admission to the hospital, the child was in poor general health, pale, and irritable. She was physically small, underdeveloped and undernourished. She had a fever of 101 degrees following routine aspirin therapy.

This child had several scars on her forehead and a prominent bruise on the left side of her scalp. Her right leg was swollen at midthigh and her right knee was swollen and deformed. Her pelvis was tender to the touch, especially in the pubic area.

Tests revealed damage to the retina of her eye. Skeletal X-rays showed old multiple fractures of her right upper leg and pelvis. There was loosening and elevation of the tissue encasing these bones, caused by ruptured blood vessels.

A CAT scan of the brain showed evidence of damage due to the application of traumatic or violent external forces. Laboratory investigations including cerebrospinal fluid examination showed evidence of iron deficiency anemia and bacterial meningitis. The diagnosis was nonaccidental injuries (child abuse) complicated by meningitis.

Does this seem like an unusual story? Each day thousands of such cases are reported. And what of the unreported cases? What of the other cases of physical neglect, and the many children who experience emotional neglect or mistreatment, most of whom are never reported to the authorities? Why do parents abuse their children? Why do reasonable, well educated, caring—if not loving—parents abuse their children?

THEORIES

The volume of literature on child abuse has increased dramatically in recent years, and information on this topic continues to accumulate rapidly. Although the act of abuse itself and the effects on the child are well documented, we know less about the circumstances surrounding abuse.

The Social Situational Model

Some researchers have explored the circumstances that produce abusive behavior.[1] Consider our way of life. We live and work in a modern, complex society, with many costly conveniences. We have cars that don't always start, and traffic jams that raise our blood pressure. We have houses with many comforts, but each comfort costs money and may break down. We have learned to live with products made by others and are indebted to those who keep them working. We have exchanged our independence for interdependence.

A lost sense of self-control often accompanies the transition to interdependence. Many people believe the result is an overwhelming feeling of frustration. If we, as adults, are caught up in a work-rush-push-and-be-pushed society, do we have the time for families? Do we have the emotional energy for families? Or, do we have to control a thin emotional line, constantly near the boiling-over point, when we face our children?

Family Life is Not a Panacea. We all carry our own emotional baggage. Family life doesn't reduce that baggage; it may add further burdens. Family life is not a panacea—a white house and picket fence with loving adults and obedient children. It is an environment rich with its own demands.

It may be impossible to understand child abuse simply by examining the social factors that affect families, or even the important psychological aspects of each family member. The factors that drive emotions vary. The advantage of using a "social situational" model to understand child abuse is that it draws from the interaction of both kinds of factors.

A bad day at the office can be mellowed by a loving greeting at the door and a wonderful evening at home. But how often does the busy two-job couple have a rested and emotionally tuned third person to meet them at the door? If everyone works, who cooks dinner and does the dishes? Words like "reasonable," "communication," "respect for," and "interest in," are important, and depict a gratifying interaction. That interaction can fail and in the process, unreasonable reactions do result even among normally reasonable people.

Patterns of Abusive Parenting

Human adjustment is not an all-or-nothing proposition. It is a combination of events, involving diverse interactions. Adjustment includes responses to friends, family, spouse, neighbors, and community. It includes reactions to the stresses of living such as monetary concerns, domestic issues, and job pressures. And there are personal issues, including drug and alcohol usage, the integration of one's personality, and even factors like satisfaction with, or distaste for, child rearing.

What are the rewards for being a successful parent? Those of us who have reared children might believe that the rewards of parenting are a green tie at Christmas (when we wear blue suits), a request for no-interest loans when the offspring is age thirty-five, and an occasional telephone call or visit if they live nearby (and most don't anymore). Most children owe a thank-you for the efforts of their parents. But it may be a long time coming, and then it may be diluted by resentments.

Parenting is an act of loving kindness, great forgiving, and even greater unselfish sharing of self. Not all human beings can be that selfless. We all require rewards for our efforts. The rewards for parenting are the pleasures of a job well done. We are rewarded by a smile, a "Mommy I love you," an "I will be good because I love you," and "Oh Dad, let me have the car. I'll be home when I promised and I will put gas in it."

Parenting has at least as many upsets and sad or angry moments as it has joyous ones. Still, the pleasure of seeing children grow and mature is a special. One new mother put it this way: "I thought that the baby would be just like me, but he was his own person, with feelings and a will from the moment he was born."

Within the recognition that each person comes into this life with a full set of needs must be the realization that each of those needs can be a parental pressure. The psychologically equipped parent expects, if not enjoys, the pressures; the ill-equipped one finds child-to-parent interactions stressful, even painful—and sometimes frightening. The results can be a negative reaction, which we term abuse or neglect.

There are three patterns of abusive parenting. First, there is the psychologically unstable and troubled parent. Second, there is the stable parent in an unstable marriage, where the pathology from the marriage or other faulty relationship spills over into the child-rearing decisions. Third, some abusive parents are psychologically adjusted but find themselves facing intractable environmental stresses.

Hours of Crisis

Typically, child abuse occurs when abnormally high frustrations, frequently unrelated to the child, reach the flare point and become anger.[2] Times of crisis are during dressing and undressing the child, especially after toileting accidents. Feeding, or other perfectly normal childhood situations where the child can produce attention-getting actions, can also cause a crisis.

One way adolescents signal that they are troubled is through a behavioral statement that draws attention to them. Only ten percent of reported cases of physically abused adolescents show other behavioral problems defined by school, community, or court standards, i.e., stealing, lying, running away, defiance.[3] The most frequent reasons for abuse cited by parents and children are: aggressive behavior (21%); lying and stealing (9%); running away, coming home late, leaving the yard without permission (7%); behavior involving food, elimination, or sleeping (7%).[4] Abuse usually occurs in response to a behavior that the parent perceives as bad or disobedient and needing to be addressed immediately. Children with handicaps—such as hyperactivity, attention deficit disorders and mental retardation—require unusual or inordinate care. They are at greater risk of physical abuse and neglect throughout the early childhood period.

An adolescent's attention-getting behaviors may be an appeal for help, but much of the attention they produce is unfavorable. Many children do not know how to ask for help. How does one say to the world, "Help me, my parents or someone else is physically abusing me, neglecting me physically, or mistreating me emotionally"? Remember that children deny mistreatment, and attempt to justify it by deserving the punishment. Often, they become victims of parental self-fulfilling prophesies. They develop attitudes of "I am bad" or "They have rejected me therefore I must be either bad or not measure up" or "If I am going to be called bad then I will act that way."

Child Abuse or Occasional Loss of Control?

Child abuse definitions highlight the risk factors important for understanding the problem and the factors that affect its increase or decline. To understand where "normal" parenting stops and child abuse begins we must be aware of current social attitudes. We must know the limits provided by public policy, agency guidelines, and legal statutes.

Any well-meaning parent can be angered to the point of losing control. If anger induces a one-time act of emotional or physical abuse, that single act does not mean the child is in a high-risk abusive environment. It may suggest that the parents need to be concerned with their own emotions and work on improving their decision-making and self-control skills.

Consider the classic Christmas film, *Angel in My Pocket*, starring Jimmy Stewart. The druggist in the movie did irreparable physical damage to the boy's hearing when he slapped him on the head. In the larger social context, that act sounds like a sure case of physical abuse. The personal context was that the druggist had just received word from the War Department that his son had died in World War II. The boy, young Jimmy Stewart's character, had correctly told the druggist that he had placed the wrong medication in the container he was filling for a customer. His drunken, angry response was to slap the boy on the ear.

In the same way, no one would consider a mother abusive who, while backing out of the driveway, accidentally runs over a two-year-old child supervised by an older sibling. In defining child abuse, behaviors cannot be separated from social and personal conditions.

The Risk Factors Change. As new information becomes available, and social attitudes change toward family, home, and child-rearing practices, the definition of abuse changes. Thus, the risk factors associated with child abuse are different today from twenty years ago. For instance, a parent can no longer take children out of school before the age of sixteen to have them work at home for any length of time without being accused of neglect and mistreatment. A few years ago that was not so. It is difficult to predict what will be considered major risk factors in another twenty years.

SOCIAL INTERPRETATIONS OF ABUSE

Child abuse must be interpreted from the social data provided by the police, courts, and professionals working with children. Differences in these interpretations produce definitions of child abuse that vary from state to state. These definitions can be classified according to the theory upon which they are based.[5]

An old and commonly applied theory is that child abuse is a form of social deviance. When child abuse is socially defined, professional and protective service providers are far more tolerant of the problem than is the public. The reason for their caution could be that when they attribute a child's condition to abuse, they may have to prove it in court. The process of proving it frequently involves the entire family, extended family, neighborhood, and community. Occasionally, the human service practitioner becomes the target of retaliatory legal actions.

Isolation

Any form of isolation, but particularly the removal of a child from the family or community support systems, may be considered emotional abuse. Some researchers go as far as to say that the isolation of children from support systems is a necessary condition in establishing child abuse.[6] A "support system" is any physical or emotional relationship that provides comfort, nutrition, protection, and security, and fosters growth or social well-being. It is also the actions by which parents, teachers, friends, and relatives guide children toward learning adult decision-making skills and self-discipline.

If a support system offers acceptance and social recognition, then isolation from that support system suggests rejection and a wide range of demeaning actions. Isolation, in a psychological sense, doesn't suggest physical isolation, which can be an effective form of punishment. Physical isolation occurs when children are placed into surroundings where they cannot attain social recognition. Emotional isolation is a form of abuse characterized by demeaning the child, which reduces feelings of self-worth and self-confidence.

Isolation and Economic Status. It was not until the 1960s that the first clinical studies reported on the relationships between the breakdown in family systems and domestic abuse and neglect. The problem behaviors associated with abusive families isolated them from the larger community and possibly other members of their families (such as grandparents, aunts and uncles, and cousins). In a study of 300 abusive families, 186 parents were chronic drinkers, 106 were psychotic, 112 had a history of at least one criminal offense, and over half the group had been tested psychologically and judged mentally retarded.[7] Eighty-five percent of the 300 families had no membership in social, religious, or other organizations. They lacked meaningful or continuing relationships with people other than immediate family members. Later work with moderate and mild child abusers has not supported the same findings as did this early work with extreme cases of child abuse. Therefore, these factors remain controversial, especially the data on alcohol use among child-abusing parents.

Follow-up studies were conducted, over a thirteen-year period, of abused children seen in a hospital.[8] The amount of time parents spent with their children, the amount of family social life, the extent of participation in community groups, the number of close friends, and the mother's feelings about how much adults could depend on the extended family were noted. Two striking findings emerged from these studies.

First, the abusive mothers were more socially isolated from any support system than were nonabusive mothers. Second, no socioeconomic differences existed between the abusive mothers and the nonabusive mothers—a finding that then was entirely unexpected.

Previously, people thought that only lower socioeconomic parents abused their children. It was unconscionable even to consider the possibility that white-collar, well-educated, middle-class families could experience child abuse. Data gathered over the last ten years has repeatedly dispelled that mistaken belief. Child abuse does not respect wealth or social status, education, or even employment.

Single-Parent Status and Child Maltreatment

Just a few years ago it was estimated that the percentage of single parents who abused their children was much higher than that of two-parent families. Research ten years ago suggested that child abuse in single-parent families was much more prevalent than recent studies show. One study found that over twenty-nine percent of physical abuse cases occurred in homes without a father or father substitute.[9] In only forty-eight percent of reported cases of physical abuse did the biological father live in the home.

In over twelve percent of the abusive families, the child's mother was absent from the home.

A 1981 national study revealed eighty-three percent of abused children were from single-parent homes (a second nonbiologically related adult also may be present in those homes).[10] The data from several studies disclosed that over half of the physically abused children came from one-parent households.

A recent study questioned adults about the physical abuse they experienced as children. Among those reporting physical abuse, twice as many had grown up in single-parent homes. The sex of the single parent was unrelated to the presence of abuse.[11] In matching neglectful parents with adequate, low-income parents, the overwhelming majority of the neglectful families had only one parent present. This is not to imply that a single parent cannot be a good parent and provide a totally nurturing home. They can, and they certainly do. But often an increasing number of stresses are felt by single parents. For example, mothers who are single parents have no one to seek emotional support from, especially in times of crisis. A major source of stress is financial worry, and this is a special problem for single mothers; they report a much lower income than do two-parent families.

Married people tend to have a more well-rounded social support system than do single parents. Not only do they have each other to depend upon, but our society is designed to accommodate married couples. It is difficult to go to parties, organizations, or even to church if everyone else there is married and you are one of the few single people present. As one single mother of two pre-school children put it, "I feel like the Lone Ranger at most social functions." The world is still arranged for pairs, and it may be a long time before this changes.

What is changing is the increasing number of support groups for single persons. To be sure, being a single parent has stresses that do not recede through sharing, but sharing is clearly a way of relieving many pressures. In any event, single parenthood is preferable to staying in a marriage with an abusive or neglectful partner.

It is a mistake to conclude that a person is a single parent due to a lack of some social, psychological, or other essential characteristic for good interpersonal relationships. While there are no data to support such assertions, they continue to be implied. It may be true that some people are without partners because they cannot enjoy any relationship or find satisfaction in any organization, and therefore become isolated. However, that is not true for all single parents.

Depression: A Cause and Consequence

A common personality characteristic of people who are isolated from social support systems is chronic or acute depression. It is difficult to say what causes depression, though personality theorists have provided us with a full array of options. Depression can lead to physical and emotional child neglect. The behaviors usually associated with depression in mothers are absence of maternal nurturing and a full range of rejecting, harsh, and punitive attitudes toward children. Depressed parents use frequent physical punishment; they are also listless, apathetic, and neglectful. Depression occurs most frequently in young mothers whose children are five years of age or younger. This is the age group that experiences the greatest amount of physical abuse. Depression is stronger in single mothers.

There is evidence, however, that depressed abusive mothers do behave differently than depressed mothers whose child-rearing practices are nonabusive.[12] Both groups of mothers were inconsistent in disciplinary techniques, alternating between expressed feelings of hostility and overprotectiveness; and both used anxiety- and guilt-inducing methods of child rearing. However, only abusive mothers used these techniques with harsh authoritarian practices.

Depression and social isolation go hand in hand. It is not easy to be certain which came first. Does depression result in isolation from support systems, or does lack of an adequate support basis produce the depression? The chicken-egg relationship between depression and isolation is even more difficult to unravel when one examines more closely the nature of interpersonal relationships of depressed and isolated child abusers.

Relationship Between Depression and Isolation. Some people believe that a common factor in isolation and depression is limited social skills, an inability to accurately read and positively react to environmental cues. Depression colors one's perceptions, and that means limited understanding of the social needs of others. In turn, failure to understand those social needs may result in poor social skills.

The question is what limited the person's social skills. There is growing recognition that, because children learn social skills early, an interrupted parent-child relationship, such as death, divorce, and abuse, may cause this problem.

Another theory is that depressed individuals drive others away. There is evidence that, just as depressive people are harsh and authoritarian toward members of their families, they may treat others the same way. Depression is difficult to treat in the adult patient and even more difficult to treat when it involves the family system.

Depression is a psychological factor, but not all reasons for social support system failure associated with child abuse are tied to a psychological variable. Some possible contributors have sociological significance. One such factor is the high rate of mobility in today's world.

Mobility

A growing body of evidence suggests that abusive parents move frequently from neighborhood to neighborhood. As a result, they do not build the same number or strength of social ties as do people who are long-term residents of a community. Years of clinical studies substantiate this belief. Residential mobility may be related to all kinds of socioeconomic and even psychological factors. According to many recent studies, frequent change of address is associated with child abuse.

A researcher reviewed 130 cases of abused children admitted to an inner-city hospital.[13] Each case was matched with the next one admitted for any other reason. Results showed that sixty-six percent of the families in the abuse group had moved within the last ten months. In contrast, only forty-two percent of the nonabusive control group had moved in the last ten months. And, sure enough, only five percent of the abusive families kept the same address over thirty months, compared to twenty percent of the control group. For single parents, residential mobility is much higher.

Again, the reasons for residential mobility, and not the mobility itself, may be the critical factors. Nonetheless, mobility often means stress in the household. While any number of risk factors may inspire child abuse, frequent changes in address foreshadow an increased likelihood of child abuse. Why? Changes in residence further reduce social interactions among families and increase isolation.

Importance of Social Systems

Most physical abuse of young children is reportedly committed by young women. Women are the primary care givers to children, especially young children. The importance social isolation plays is not yet well documented, but let's examine it hypothetically. A young woman with few friends or social contacts within the community must stay home all day with several small children. That evening her husband comes home, eats, changes clothes, and leaves to be with his friends. She feels deserted and alone, tired of being confined at home and with the society of small children. Her feelings turn to anger. Instead of responding with patience and reason to one of her children's undesirable behaviors, she reacts in anger.

Child abuse, in this scenario, may be explained by the frustration-aggression theory. Children are rejected by an overburdened mother who feels and, often is, alone, even if she has a mate. Children also may bear the effects of the anger she feels either for her husband or for the world. She cannot strike out at her husband or the world. But she can strike her children. In one study, mothers who were home all day were more likely to reject their children than were mothers who had the company of another adult, especially one with no child-rearing responsibilities.[14]

Recent research supports this theory.[15] Over one thousand parents responded to a self-disclosure questionnaire on child abuse. Families who did not belong to organizations, who attended church less than once each year, and whose nearest relative was more than an hour away reported the most frequent abuse. What constitutes an adequate social support system is not fully understood, but there is evidence that one is needed. Parenting without a good support base, especially for young parents or single parents who carry additional social or psychological stresses, strongly increases the probability of child abuse.

The type of support base available has also been studied.[16] According to one study, abusive mothers had as many friends as did nonabusive mothers, but had fewer relatives and neighbors they considered "family." Abusive mothers rarely saw relatives, and few lived nearby; they did not see their kin even once each year (the standard used in the study).

In a study of loneliness in abusive families, the close physical proximity of families was unrelated to loneliness.[17] Loneliness was generally self-imposed. It was a psychological detachment associated with a fear of being hurt emotionally by friends and even relatives. A major finding was that this self-imposed loneliness was a result of poor social skills. These people were unable—or believed themselves unable—even to participate in neighborly exchanges of goods and services.

Personality and Social Isolation. Adults' inability to seek and use social support systems, rather than the simple lack of availability of friends, relatives, and neighbors, differentiates them from others in a community neighborhood. Eight personality characteristics can isolate family members and place the family at risk for child abuse. These are:

1. An overwhelming belief that nothing is worth doing;
2. The presence of emotional numbness, hopelessness, despondency, and despair;

3. Superficial emotional relationships and intense loneliness;
4. An absence of social living skills;
5. Passive-aggressive expressions of anger;
6. General feelings of apathy and negativism;
7. Poorly developed decision-making skills and the inability to think through a problem; and
8. Seeing futility in others and in having a relationship with others.

PARENT-CHILD INTERACTIONS

Recently, a thirty-two-year-old man was acquitted of abusing his twenty-three-month-old daughter. He dipped her feet into scalding hot water drawn into the bath tub while trying to bathe her. His defense was that he did not know that she could be burned so easily.

The relationships between parents and children are many and various. What defines the nature of a parent-to-child and child-to-parent relationship? Is there a standard established by tradition or recommended by the professional community?

The accepted belief that children are takers and parents are givers has a strong economic tone, and it is not altogether true. The strength of the bond between parents and child depends on the values of the parent. Parents and families place various values on children. In many larger families, children have been reared by older siblings. In some affluent homes, nannies have reared the children. In poor homes, with working single parents, baby-sitters or grandparents have done the job. There are parents who place a low value on children and child-rearing. It is difficult for them to see themselves as care givers. Children may be viewed as a financial burden, or they may be seen as a necessary, though not completely wanted, means for the family to receive an income from a social service agency.

As they develop, children need to interact both socially and psychologically, adding to the richness of the family. Children require a family to decide its priorities by declaring its values. If wealth is judged important, then family size may be a factor. If human interaction is judged to be important, and strong, independent people the goal, then material things may be less important.

Recently a father revealed that he was going through a real bout with depression. His youngest child, who had lived at home throughout college, was leaving to take a job. This family had reared eight children on a professor's salary. Two of these children had already become physicians. This is an example of a child-oriented family where mutual acceptance and a two-way positive relationship had achieved a deep and rich meaning.

Human development is a process by which children learn to adapt to the society in which they live.[18] Societal demands differ from stage to stage; normal development suggests that children master certain skills at each stage. A most important skill is human interaction. Abusive punishment, emotional abuse, or poorly defined and inconsistent disciplinary practices threaten both bonding and human interaction skill development.

Children and Conflicting Values

Children represent conflict in adult values from before birth. Outside forces, such as religion, insert different values that may be inconsistent with individual beliefs. For example, some religions support large families, while others consider birth control a personal decision. Exterior value systems may well override personal decisions, resulting in unwanted children.

Having lost the locus of control even before birth, parents may view the child as an unwanted interloper presented to them by an unfeeling and unsympathetic higher order. The child becomes the object of resentments that cannot be expressed toward the church. Parents who begin child rearing with this viewpoint probably will gain little satisfaction from the experience. Frequently they become emotionally cold, indifferent, rigid, and even rejecting and neglectful of their children.

Bonding and Parenting Instincts

We assume that parental bonding is automatic and instinctive, occurring during moments of close contact just after birth. Within that assumption is the belief that parent-child relationships are wholesome, healthy, nurturing, caring, positive experiences. Actually, many child-parent relationships are low in trust. Some are emotionally painful and others actually inflict physical pain or discomfort.

In the nineteenth century, behaviorists began to question the existing belief that instinct directed many human behaviors.[19] It was once thought that parenting was mostly instinctive. Today, we believe that it is primarily learned behavior, although there are, clearly, instinctive behaviors. For instance, newborns seem to appear ready to eat, and eating means sucking, which is an instinctive behavior. But not all children are drawn to a loving breast. Children born with fetal alcohol syndrome may be born drunk and mentally retarded. Life for others will be full of uncertainties, even in terms of who next will feed them, shelter them, or clothe them. We speak of parent-child bonding as if it were a steel weld. But bonding may be interfered with by many physical or environmental circumstances, or it may not occur at all.

Another earlier belief was that there was an instinctive relationship between mother and child. Recent data does suggest that physiology changes occur in preparation for delivery. There are pregnancy-related behavioral changes. Increased hormonal responses, and what we now recognize as the need for mothers to receive stimuli from their newborn, are two such factors. Data from several studies suggest that the more prolonged the early neonatal relationship, the stronger the child-mother bond. In fact, the early relationship between the parent and child, and the tone of the relationship, appear in "bout-initiation," or the rewards provided the care giver by the child. Very little is known about this aspect of the parent-child relationship.

The parent-to-child bond is not a simple one-way street. Beginning before birth, children are already being programmed for success or failure depending upon the prevailing feelings of the pregnant parents. As animals prepare, so must human beings. Among animals, though, raising newborns is usually a matter of weeks. Even a two-ton elephant weans its offspring in two years. Lower animals raise their young to physical independence. When the young can find food, can defend themselves, and can fly, hide, or run, they are forced from the nest. In humans, this process is much more sophisticated, with schools, social agencies, and exterior value systems dictating child-rearing norms to young parents.

In short, many factors influence the assumed strength of parental-child relationships, not the least of which is the child. Mothers often compare children, remarking that one child was easy to rear, while another was difficult. They do not intend to imply that they are rejecting or less loving of the more difficult child, but probably they simply appreciate the more rewarding child. I have heard mothers explain that a certain child was "very easy to love."

There is not yet much data on what children provide to the parenting relationship. The perception of the child's presence seems to fall on a continuum ranging from total acceptability of child-for-mother and mother-for-child to a range of lowered trust, even mistrust.

Baby apes select cloth mothers over wire mothers, suggesting the need for a soft and responsive stimulus. In like manner, human infants seem to have an unexplained affinity for particular people, not necessarily the parent. There are people—and frequently they are men—who can pick up any crying baby and it will invariably stop crying. Why does such a peculiar bonding occur? There is much we do not know about how infants and children form relationships with adults in general and parents in particular.

Scientific inquiry into the response of parents to children is still on the threshold. There is some evidence to suggest that a range of temperaments exists in newborns. It seems that the infant-parent interaction is not any different from any other relationship. There must be need-recognition and need-satisfaction or the relationship may experience discomfort that interferes with the bonding process.

SUMMARY

This chapter asks why child abuse occurs. It raises issues associated with abuse and exposes the conditions under which abuse occurs. Child abuse has many contributing causes. For some, it is an outgrowth of too much, occurring much too frequently—an inability to cope adequately with modern life's stressors. For others, child abuse is a quick response to an irritant. For a few, it represents an extreme and pathological response.

What this chapter established was the need for mutual satisfactions in marriage and family life resulting in growth experiences. What this chapter recommends is that most human beings need assistance with the pressures of life, and especially with the added pressures of child rearing. Child rearing, under the best of conditions, requires hard and dedicated work. Under unsettled home conditions it can become a turmoil that exaggerates feelings. The result is a loss of adult self-control.

The good news is that parents respond well to training. Those who don't may require additional support to empower them to deal with the conditions that threaten their well-being. When we feel inadequate, we lower our expectancies for our own performance. A cycle of disruptive parenting may begin, ending in the tragedy of abuse. The results of support groups and family therapy for domestic violence problems have been encouraging and offer a great deal of hope.

ATTACHMENT OR NEGLECT?
The Parent-Child Relationship

A child
is a person who is going
to carry on what you have started
He is going
to sit where you are sitting
and when you are gone
attend to those things
which you think are important
You may adopt
all the policies you please
but how they are carried on
depends on him
He will
assume control of your
cities, states, and nations
He is going
to move in and take over
your churches, schools, universities,
and corporations
The fate of humanity
is in his hands.

Abraham Lincoln

TOO LITTLE, BUT NOT TOO LATE

Many consider our nation to be the richest on earth. Yet, despite material success, the American family is in trouble. Family mobility, chemical dependence, displaced workers, changes in roles within the family, and domestic violence have all challenged the twentieth century American family. Those who pay the heaviest price for this family disruption are the children.

The Dream and the Reality

Children's physical and emotional growth and development depends on the type and amount of nurturing they receive. Generally, society considers the physical and personality growth of children so basic that it assumes the adult world will not misuse children. To most adults, the thought of failing to protect and shield children—of not providing a physically and emotionally secure world—is inconceivable. That fact explains some issues related to how children find their way into crisis.

It is possible that we make more assumptions about child rearing than any other human endeavor. Child rearing, as a psychosocial event within the home, is clearly a thread that is continuously woven into the social tapestry. That is why the parenting act is relative to the social and personal scheme of things at any given time. The structure of emotional interactions creating the bond between parents and child is extremely complex.

We assume that parents will love and protect their children, providing an ever-present nurturing relationship. We also assume that all children are born into a friendly environment, not a hostile one, and that children will receive love and emotional nurturing from the day of their birth to the day they leave the parent's protective shelter. Within the parent-child relationship, there are two competing forces——the dream and reality.

The Dream. The romantic notions of family life and child rearing go as follows: A wonderfully stable young man with well-developed values and a successful career with a bright future marries an attractive young woman who is full of kindness, understanding, and the wish to dedicate herself to her husband and yet-unborn children. They share a secure love that is rich, kind, forgiving, abundant, and always present. They are there for each other and whosoever enters their home. They are eager to have a family, one boy and one girl. Each child will have a room, and the parents place college monies into a special savings account even before the children are conceived. The grandparents live in the same town and so do aunts and uncles, nieces and nephews. It is a time of peace, family fun, and wonderful vacations. It is a time to grow and develop healthy bodies and sound minds.

Furthermore, in our dream, all children are born healthy, happy, and easy to manage. All children instinctively love their parents and attempt to do just what Mommy and Daddy expect of them. They will grow up eager to respond positively to their parents' expectations of them. They will never challenge, threaten, lie, or deceive their parents. Their parents will have a very special place in their hearts all the days of their lives. In this perfect world there are no handicapped children, not even hyperactive ones who begin life with excessive colic and inability to sleep at night. In this perfect world every child shows appreciation for the parents' love, repaying it measure for measure, by making the world a better place in which to live.

The social order is protective of children. There are no drug dealers at the edge of the playground. There is no alcohol in the cupboard. Father and mother are always there, for Little League, Cub Scouts and Brownies, school programs and parent-teacher conferences, and to supply enriched social and informational learning experiences at each step of the way. There is no reason for child labor laws, and prime time television each evening is the *Family Channel* and *Discovery*. Teachers are respectful and creative, support learning and develop children's abilities. In the history of a rich community resource of children's activities never has there been physical or sexual abuse or neglect.

The social order recognizes the importance of the next generation, and is respectful of its promise. The adult model is emotionally warm, stable, and conveys a deep, abiding respect for the environment, the resources of this land, and for others who are different. A major effort exists to provide for deficiencies in the relative wealth among people, offering dental, medical, home and family support, food, shelter and clothing. Should a child or family experience the need for assistance, a social blanket of psychological and economic nurturing is readily available through community agencies and governmental departments.

The Reality. But, for many people, life offers little advanced planning. It offers few opportunities to be prepared, to anticipate what is going to happen. For many, life is long stretches of boredom interrupted with brief periods of crisis. The periods of boredom are frequently filled with fears, possible isolation, external and internal struggles to control one's being. These lead to periods of open conflict, generally with authority figures at home, school, work, or in the community.

A fifteen-year-old girl, whose mother has been married three times, is facing the fifth "live in" boyfriend since the last stepfather five years ago. She is average in intelligence and received good grades up until the sixth grade. After that she failed to see any purpose to school. As her grades failed, so did her ability to develop friendships.

Several of her former girlfriends were in different class sections, and since they live on the other side of town, she seldom sees them socially. Her new friends were poor students in lower academic achievement sections. These students were often from broken homes, had poor grades, and several were already known to the authorities.

She constantly disagreed with her mother, and her mother's new boyfriend about her mother. Her siblings were too young to provide her much support, and no relatives lived in the community. She did not belong to any clubs or sponsored after-school activities. She had never been in church, Brownies, or Girl Scouts. She had never been in music or organized sports, though she loved both activities. She was frustrated by the fact that she could not have music lessons. The music teacher at school had kicked her and her group out of music class and music club. She loved sports but fared no better in any type of organized sports activity.

At fifteen she was alone, hating school, isolated from the things she wanted and surrounded by people and things she didn't want. At fifteen she met Eddie. Eddie was twenty-five and a loner, well known by the courts, job service and social agencies. He could not keep a job. He had no formal training. Like her, he was frustrated and angry. Like her, he was alone and without goals and directions. Like her, he dreamed of a brighter tomorrow, only to find that morning brought fears, uncertainties and more frustration.

Their relationship was ordinary. They had no money. They liked to walk and talk. They both enjoyed the escape that beer and drugs brought to them. They both felt briefly secure and attached, confusing love and sexual gratification. She got pregnant. He got a job in California. At sixteen she has a baby boy who was born chemically dependent. The boy is not yet two but is hyperactive and suffering from significant developmental delays in speech and motor development.

She continues to live at home where she is clearly unwanted. She is depressed and unable to cope. The baby cries too much, and needs too many things she cannot provide. She takes a job at night in an all-night diner waiting tables. Her fourteen-year-old sister watches the baby. The sister entertains friends, and during the "drug" party the baby screams for his mother. The boys at the party put their cigarettes out on the baby, and slap it to make it stop crying. When it won't, one boy hits it repeatedly.

When she comes home the baby is in the hospital and she is charged with child abuse.

In 1987 the *American Humane Association* reported two million cases of maltreatment of children (includes physical abuse, sexual abuse, and emotional neglect and mistreatment). It is reasonable to assume that the actual number of cases of emotional neglect far exceeds that figure. Most human service agencies believe neglect—generally defined as no nurturing parental attachment—is underreported.

In recent years, we have developed a sensitivity to physical and sexual abuse. We recognize that over a half million children annually suffer physical abuse at the hands of their parents. Of that number, four thousand die. Citizens see physical and emotional abuse as both a major social and a major community problem. Much less emphasis is placed on neglect and emotional mistreatment factors such as alcohol use, failure to provide, and educational neglect. The awareness and reporting of overt physical and sexual abuse is increasing rapidly, especially since the law of the land now requires it. It is difficult not to report and investigate a child with cigarette burns. It is difficult not to report alleged reports of sexual abuse, including fondling. But in case of failure to thrive it is much more difficult to gain the attention of human service protective agencies and to obtain relief in the courts.

THE BOUNDARIES OF EMOTIONAL NEGLECT

Failure to Thrive

"Failure to thrive" is a term pediatricians use to describe a child who is born healthy but then begins to fall below the standard measures of growth. Failure to thrive may be caused by physical disease, or by neglect or mistreatment. Reasons for failure to thrive may be as simple as feeding errors. Other reasons stem from complex factors including: faulty mother-infant bonding, the mother's psychological status, family dysfunction, environmental stresses, and forced separation and dependency. An example of the latter is when children refuse food or display other attention-getting behaviors to express anger and assert independence in an attempt to manipulate parental actions.

Emotional Abuse

Physical abuse occurs most often when the family is in crisis.[1] Circumstances that have preceded fatal attacks include colic and toilet training failures. By contrast, the more subtle behaviors associated with emotional abuse may be seen in the parents' language or in their limited or guarded interactions with their children.

Emotional abuse also appears in traditional controls instilling fear. The number of fear-induced tales that parents use to control children is alarming. Frequently these stories include bogeymen, snakes, monsters, or other horrors. They are meant to keep children safe from harm by keeping them in at night, away from rivers or fires, and away from dangerous people. But an unwanted result is that children grow up with unrealistic fears. Although some use of this controlling folklore is a common child-rearing practice, extreme or ghastly stories are very frightening to children.

For years, most observers of child development have been reporting on the impact of poor family relationships.[2] Adults who did not grow up with the comfort and support of a nurturing emotional relationship often display lifelong psychological problems. Their behaviors range from antisocial to self-destructive.

Parent training and stronger support systems in the eighteen- to twenty-four-month age period are critical in preventing child abuse and neglect.[3] Parents in one study were longing for information to give them a different approach to parent-child interactions.

Although we can estimate how often physical and sexual abuse occurs, we have no idea about the scope of emotional neglect—in the United States, or the world. We also have only limited knowledge about the range of neglectful actions practiced with children. Lacking a tight definition of emotional neglect, it is unclear where emotional neglect begins and ends. This makes human service case work a morass of lawsuits.

A case in point is a 1988 definition offered by a West Virginia Abuse Prevention Project; it does not differentiate between abuse and neglect.[4] This definition states:

Child Abuse and Neglect: Physical injury, substantial mental or emotional injury, sexual abuse, sexual exploitation, or negligent treatment or maltreatment of a child by a parent, guardian or custodian who is responsible for the child's welfare, under circumstances that harm or threaten the health and welfare of the child.

Contrast an expanded definition from Tennessee:

Dependent or Neglected child means a child:

(a) Who is without a parent, guardian or legal custodian;
(b) Whose parent, guardian, or person with whom the child lives, by reason of cruelty, mental incapacity, immorality, or depravity is unfit to properly care for such a child;
(c) Who is under unlawful or improper care, supervision, custody or restraint by any person, corporation, agency, association, institution, society or

other organization or who is unlawfully kept out of school;

(d) Whose parent, guardian or custodian neglects or refuses to provide necessary medical, surgical, institutional or hospital care for such child;

(e) Who because of lack of proper supervision is found in any place the existence of which is in violation of the law;

(f) Who is in such condition of want or suffering or is under improper guardianship or control as to injure or endanger the morals or health of himself or others;

(g) Who is suffering from or has sustained a wound, injury, disability, or physical or mental condition caused by brutality, abuse or neglect;

(h) Who has been in the care and control of an agency or person who is not related to such child by blood or marriage for a continuous period of eighteen months or longer in the absence of a court order and such person or agency has not initiated judicial proceedings seeking either legal custody or adoption of the child; or

(i) Who is or has been allowed, encouraged or permitted to engage in prostitution or obscene or pornographic photographing, filming, posing, or similar activity and whose parent, guardian or other custodian neglects or refuses to protect such child from further such activity.

These two examples show how varied definitions of neglect can be. The West Virginia definition ties neglect to abuse. The one used by Tennessee offers specific statements about socially condemned forms of neglect, such as sexual exploitation. It is clear from these examples how difficult it is to try to define the emotional communication and nurturing that can be measured in parent-child attachments. Yet these qualities are important to human growth and development.

Defining Emotional Neglect by What it is Not

Many people have studied how social awareness of problems changes.[5] For example, not until medical evidence proved that physical abuse was occurring could a significant level of social conscience develop. Many factors affect the speed and degree with which society will act upon a problem. Among these are gender, family role stereotypes, abuse of power, the ability of society to compensate for perceived powerlessness, similar social and psychological effects on the victim, and the relationship between types of abuse and types of families.

The problem may be that we have tried to define emotional neglect in the same way as physical or sexual abuse. Those definitions require confirming evidence that physical or sexual abuse has occurred. In the same way, legislators and human service professionals are now attempting to define emotional neglect according to what should occur. The social and personal development of all children should be noted as the child grows. When it falls short of the norm, then human service intervention with families could occur.

The point is that emotional neglect is not, like physical or sexual abuse, the presence of unwanted or inappropriate actions. It is the absence of attachment. Neglect shows up in two forms: (1) the child's development may be disturbed, or (2) abnormal responses may appear, by the child, the parent, or in the parent-child relationship. Today we assume that parents are giving their children healthy experiences during social and personal growth. No one intervenes unless something unfavorable draws our attention to the situation. That form of intervention, after the fact, is "too little, too late."

Emotional neglect generally must have one or more of four components in order for it to be recognized. Those four factors are: (1) failure to educate, which generally involves not sending children to school; (2) failure to supervise properly children's home and street activities; (3) failure to offer needed medical care, or social services, if outlined by a community agency as important; and (4) the absence of appropriate food and shelter. These omissions are clearly mistreatment, and indicate neglect. They do not define emotional neglect or abuse, as most loving and caring parents would describe it.

Quality is the Key Word

Researchers usually focus on the following eight categories of abuse: (1) physical abuse, (2) sexual abuse, (3) emotional mistreatment, (4) nutritional neglect, (5) medical neglect, (6) supervision, (7) cleanliness, and (8) housing. In surveys that ask different people to classify behaviors according to these categories, several interesting findings appear. Sexual abuse and medical neglect items are easily and reliably classified. Physical abuse is clouded by disciplinary issues. As expected, there is much confusion about the failure to provide supervision and about emotional maltreatment. It is simply not easy to judge the quality of a child's supervision as it applies to emotional care. The key word is quality; the judgment is about the quality of the parent-child relationship.

Let's examine the primary factors associated with emotional neglect.

Isolation. Abusive adults do not have friends and adult personal relationships. They frequently force children to become more dependent, in compensation, or they may neglect the attachment to children as they do adult relationships.

Lack of Support. A major finding about abusive parents is that they are unable to connect with outside support systems even when they are available.

Marital Problems. The absence of supportive relationships extends to spousal relationships.

Life Crisis. Abusive parents are frequently overcome by losses: losses of employment, housing, sufficient food, clothing; they live in futility.

Lack of Ability to Care for Others. Some parents, overwhelmed with life's stresses, are unable to respond to others. Frequently I have heard, "I don't have anything to give."

Lack of Child-Rearing Skills. Often neglectful parents either don't know they are neglectful or could not do anything about it if they did. Training in parenting skills appears to help, often forming a support base for parents.

THE MALTREATMENT-MALTREATING CYCLE

The maltreatment-maltreating cycle is the most striking example of the continuation of learned behaviors. It was not until 1969 that the theory of attachment as a principal emotional and developmental learning system across the generations was first proposed.[6] Later studies found that maltreating parents minimize or downplay their childhood maltreatment. Frequently, on surface inquiry, these parents report their childhood only as a pleasant experience, with two of the most sensitive questions being: (1) Did anyone who cared for you beat you up? and (2) How were you punished as a child? It is simply not good enough to continue to believe that adult behaviors do not reflect childhood experiences regarding relationships.

Characteristics of Neglectful Parents

To paraphrase Jonathan Livingston Seagull, a seeker must become a finder and eventually a giver.[7] Parental neglect is a tragic story. It is the absence of parental giving and the result is faulty attachments or parent-child relationships. Neglect affects all of the children's development including the type of emotional response they will offer to their children when they become parents.

Do neglectful parents share specific personality types? Early studies reported that neglectful parents were easily upset, unstable emotionally, and angry, often feeling isolated and alone.[8] Maltreating care providers are frequently frightened by external (to the family and home) threats and controls. Some studies have found that abusive parents expressed more annoyance and less sympathy in response to infant distress.[9] They were less attentive to children's needs, more consumed by their own, and simply not responsive to children's emotional conditions. They lacked awareness of the social information-processing signal system used by children, and often lacked the appropriate social response tools used by nonabusive parents.

Maltreating parents report that children "get on their nerves" and are difficult to manage; they consider the home as a stressful, not a secure or comfortable, place. Maltreating mothers see their children's needs differently than mothers of other children. Their response is exactly opposite to that of nonneglectful parents. They tend to believe that their own children have stable internal characteristics and can handle unstable environments or situations. Other people's children do not have this internal stability and need and deserve a highly stable environment.

The faulty perceptions that maltreating parents have of their children has become a major new avenue for research.[10] There is evidence that parents have internal working models of the parent-child interaction, and these models are faulty, in response to their childhood parent-child relationship. Parents successful in care giving are sensitive and make loving support and emotional responsiveness available; they experience a high sense of self-esteem and confidence while giving. Maltreating parents have erroneous models of the parent-child relationship and what parent-child interactions mean. The type of feedback they receive from parenting is probably negative or limited and directly correlates with what they put into the relationship.

Attachment Disorders

Emotional neglect is an attachment disorder in which a care giver (1) does not know how to nurture a child, (2) is unable psychologically to nurture, or (3) is unwilling psychologically to nurture. These three factors form a loose-knit relationship, and cannot be considered in isolation from one another. Dysfunctional families, rejection, stress, and separation problems often intensify attachment disorders.

Dysfunctional Family. When parents become preoccupied with themselves and their problems there may be little nurturing of children. Among the most common and best documented are care givers who have histories of child abuse, neglect, and deprivation. Adults having suffered these problems are often depressed and unable to bring their feelings to the surface and share them.[11]

Rejection. Few parents practice outright exclusion of their children; many events and circumstances either make the bonding a positive experience or set rejection into motion. Some of these are the child's appearance, personality, ease of care, and response to parents. A frequently rejected group is handicapped children. Other common cause of parental rejection are hyperactivity and mental retardation.

Stress. A new infant can overburden a family that has little holding it together. Caring for young children is stressful, especially when there are many others. The stress of child rearing is multiplied when employment, money, inadequate housing, health problems, poor extended family relationships, and poor parental relationships exist.

Separation Disorders. Separation disorders occur later in the child's development. One outstanding characteristic of a separation disorder is that there is constant negotiation going on between child and parent. Often, the items the child attempts to negotiate are ones that should not even be open for negotiation. Often they are inappropriate displays of behavior that distort everyday eating, drinking, bathing, going to school, toileting, playing.

Types of Attachments

Emotional sensitivity to the needs of the newborn and the nurturing response to those needs should provide the basis for a secure attachment. Research has generally established three types of child responses to care givers: (1) secure attachment, (2) anxious-avoidant, and (3) anxious-ambivalent.

Secure Attachments. Infants are born displaying two emotional responses: distress and delight. The continuous unfolding of these responses into a full spectrum of distinctive emotions is emotional maturation and it defines emotional adjustment. There is strong evidence that the psychological maturity and emotional adjustment of any adult is related to the bond between that adult as a child and a primary care giver.

Estimates suggest that about seventy percent of the children in this country have secure attachments to their care givers and grow in emotional maturity. The ability to define and seek comfort, solve problems, and make decisions that generate comfort is what defines psychological maturity. This is an important definition. Included in the definition is the fact that psychological adjustment is a lifelong experience.

Anxious-Avoidant Attachments. Anxious-avoidant infants cannot depend on the care giver to meet their needs responsively. This group is at the center of the problem of physical and emotional neglect. The degree of emotional neglect has been a question of considerable importance and remains a major issue that research has not answered. An example might be a parent (particularly a mother) who is emotionally unstable, possibly chemically dependent, or absent from the child or home for extended periods of time.

Anxious-Ambivalent Attachments. The third group of infants is characterized as anxious-ambivalent. Even in the presence of the parent, they are unable to find comfort and calm down when distressed. They experience mixed responses from the care givers, and the care giver may even resist their needs. Their mothers seem unable to show positive emotions consistently. They are highly inconsistent in responding to their children. Both the anxious-avoidant and anxious-ambivalent responses of children are thought to be caused by maltreatment from the care giver resulting in a disorganized/disoriented attachment.[12]

Fear can be the basis of both physical and emotional abuse in children. Disoriented attachments are a strong conflict resulting from the child's simultaneous approach to the care giver for comfort and retreat for safety. Mothers with affective disorders—especially those with clinical depression—were the single highest contributors to disorganized attachment relationships.

Male Versus Female Attachments. One recent finding is that there is a high preponderance of insecure attachments among male infants as compared to female infants.[13] The presence of a male spouse or partner in the home had a different effect on attachment security for boys than girls in lower socioeconomic circumstances. The absence of the father figure seriously jeopardized the infant male-mother attachment relationships. This finding suggests that if the parents' relationship is bad, or if the father is absent, or if there is domestic violence, greater opportunity exists for the mother to express hostility toward the male child.

Impressions of Adversity

Only in the last decade has research on the effects of adverse childhood experiences on the development of self, social relationships and psychopathology occurred in earnest. A major theory of this work is that the healthy development of children depends on a secure early attachment to a primary care giver.

There is ample evidence now that a lack of strong emotional support and interaction in infancy not only alters emotional growth but also influences all behavioral development. Several studies have shown that the absence of early emotional development leads to poor social, emotional, cognitive, and representative skills in later life.

Most people agree that the quality of a child's peer relationships stems directly from the bond to the primary care giver in infancy.[14] Children who feel positive emotions from these care givers build models in which they see themselves as worthy of the concern of others. Studies have shown that the quality of the bond between care giver and child affects emotional development in preschool and academic performance and social/personal growth in the school-age period. There is even evidence that emotional neglect during childhood may later appear in adult life as mental health disorders.

TRIGGERS OF EMOTIONAL ABUSE AND NEGLECT

There is a sharp contrast between the occurrence of physical abuse and emotional neglect.[15] Physical abuse generally occurs in the presence of trivial irritants. Some common triggers are messy feedings, soiling, and intractable crying. The purpose of the resulting punishment is frequently to curb behavior the parent saw as inappropriate.

The same is not true for emotional neglect. The most common reason for the emotional neglect of children is conflict between adults. The frustration and anger between adults appears to spill over into the adult-child relationship. Often parents simply redirect their frustration and anger toward the child. Other significant reasons are poor parenting skills and lack of knowledge about the child's needs. There are generally no child-related reasons or immediate environmental triggers for emotional neglect.

Often what exists within the parent is the so-called "apathy-futility" syndrome. That simply is the parent's lack of motivation to provide the type of emotional environment essential to a child's development. The question becomes: How can parents convey positive emotions to their children when they do not feel those emotions or, even if they feel them, do not have the energy to express them? Then too, parents may not realize the vital need children have, beginning at birth, to be totally immersed in a positive emotional interaction. The next question then is what occurs if the parent's emotional response is negative, or if it is simply not there.

Emotional Neglect is Ongoing

Physical abuse is rarely a daily occurrence. By contrast, emotional neglect usually is a continuing reaction, tending to occur with regularity. Emotional neglect does not seem to cycle; there is rarely the opposite emotional interchange or even a "honeymoon period" such as frequently follows physical or sexual abuse.

Physical or sexual abuse may be a limited interaction, occurring rarely between an adult and one or two of the children. In physical or sexual abuse, other family members may also punish the recipient or they may attempt to offer unusually strong emotional support systems. Emotional neglect is usually more family-wide, chronic, and it often reflects perverse interpersonal conflict, apathy, and irresponsibility.

Physical abuse is likely to create a cycle of future hostile interactions as the abused child grows into adulthood. Cases of sexual abuse show a classic cycle of justification into the next generation. But emotional neglect and abuse threaten a major developmental part of life. Its influence is continuous, ongoing throughout the life span and touching all aspects of development.

How can physical or sexual abuse occur without emotional abuse? It appears that more than one type of abuse may occur in a family at any single time. There is, however, evidence that emotional neglect may be the most common form of faulty parent-child interaction. As one caseworker put it, "yes is yes, no is no, and emotional neglect is maybe."

TEENS AT RISK

Adolescents who are emotionally abused and neglected by their parents are members of the at-risk group in our society. They are at risk of committing suicide; of becoming pregnant, chemically dependent, school and social system failures; and of developing court records.

The at-risk factors for emotionally abused and neglected teens are:

- drug and alcohol involvement
- promiscuous sexual activity
- increased medical problems
- increased mental illness (i.e., phobias, depression, personality disorders, psychosis)
- family violence
- child neglect and abuse
- running away of children and parents
- criminal activity
- hopelessness, despondency, depression
- suicide

Estimates suggest that well over a million children are emotionally mistreated or neglected each year.[16] Adolescence is a particularly critical time for maltreatment to occur; twice the neglect occurs after age eleven than before age six. About 300,000 cases of adolescent neglect are reported, but authorities believe that nearly forty percent of the worst cases are not reported.

Parents who give security to infants or young children may feel threatened as the children grow into adolescents. The emotional development of neglected teenagers comes to a standstill just when they need family support most and should be developing a strong sense of values regarding self-worth and responsibility in the treatment of others. Instead, what happens is neglect passes from one generation to the next. Non-nuturing parents may begin with neglect, then resort to using excessive physical or psychological controls.

Control issues become exaggerated between parent and adolescent with disciplinary measures, too often, having a negative effect on family unity and support. Disagreement between parents about appropriate discipline for adolescents expands. There is greater opportunity for step-parent/stepchild dysfunction as the child moves into adolescence. Teens in conflict with their parents show less reasoning and greater stress reactions with more frequent serious adjustment conflicts.

The rise in juvenile crime may be related to parental neglect.[17] Three observations point to the neglect-delinquency connection. First, neglected children generally show aggression. Second, families of neglected children and families of known delinquents have the same disruptions in family relations. Third, approximately fifteen percent of neglected children are arrested during their teenage years.

WHAT WE MUST DO

As this nation enters the twenty-first century, it can ill afford to waste any of its resources. If the United States is to remain a competitive economy and democratic nation, all areas of society must appreciate the vital importance of our children.

It is now time to make a choice about our behavior on this planet. That choice will be whether we will live together, in search of solutions for the common good, or perish. We can declare "wars on drugs"—but we are not winning. Drugs themselves are not the issue. The issue is that the sale of drugs in this country is dependent on the demand of a buyer. Society must stop attempting to do to and for people. The conflicts and pressures on the American value system concerning family responsibility are huge.

We can no longer consider control and force as appropriate and necessary means to produce the behaviors we want. We must replace control and force with values that will promote children's understanding of themselves, respect for others, and understanding and respect for nature.

What is the aim as we help the child toward maturity? We want a person who feels self-worth; who has self-discipline; who knows right from wrong; who does not yield to harmful desires. We want a child who feels responsibility to preserve the creatures, plants, soil, water, and air on this planet. Children will only learn this from those around them.

> *Let us take up stones*
> *that people are ready*
> *to throw at each other*
> *and put them down*
> *for our children to walk on.*
>
> Bruce W. Patalano
> Wheeling, WV

For physical abuse, our efforts must focus on creating an effective parent-child interaction. The focus of interventions in emotional cruelty must attempt to improve the quality of adult interactions and reduce conflict between adults. The apathy-futility syndrome, or neglect, requires long-term commitment to education or reeducation and total community support of the family unit. Clearly, the traditional role of agencies must change from that of identifying and relieving an individual client's needs to viewing the family as a unit.

The Need for Human Support

The need for adequate support systems for all people, particularly neglected children in nonfunctioning or dysfunctional families, is a major issue facing our society now. How much longer will we deal with human needs by control and force? When will we learn how to deal with human beings? If, metaphorically speaking, life is a journey, when rough spots in the road appear, we all need a few essentials:

> *That in getting through*
> *a rough time*
> *we need three things.*
> *Something to do*
> *Something or someone to love and*
> *Something to look forward to.*
> Joseph Addison

I believe that the most important consideration in measuring a child's psychological status is the type and amount of human support the child has. Human support means having access to a problem-solving process. How critical to life that someone be there for us, and how much is lost when we have no one to love and with whom to share ourselves! The most elementary ingredient in the human relationship experience is that emotion called love, which can be defined as a bottomless cup of kindness and forgiveness.

Greater awareness is sorely needed in several areas:

Educating Professionals. Not all professional people yet recognize emotional neglect in children or families.

Interagency Cooperation. It is not unusual for several agencies to work simultaneously with one family. Too often they have no interagency communications and no cooperation. It is even possible to find two or more agencies offering different interventions simultaneously to the same parent.

Parent Education. This is the most necessary item. Generally, when people receive information they behave differently. Parents simply need information. Sometimes they need assistance, and sometimes they need to hear the problem and see that there are solutions. Sometimes parents don't know about community resources that are available to them. Parents need help with the details of child rearing. Parents need to know that others may have faced the same problem.

Parental Support Groups. Parents must know that they are not alone in their struggle.

Family as a Support Structure. From time to time the immediate or extended family can be a support system.

Sometimes parents are afraid to ask for what would really help them.

Six Steps We Must Take

Step 1. Identify the factors that cause neglect by studying the family system, looking first at the history of the parents and their behaviors. Observing the interaction and relationship between parent and child should be part of this step. The quantity and quality of communications between parent and child are particularly important.

Step 2. Replace unwanted parent behaviors and nonnurturing environmental circumstances with those that enhance positive parent-child attachment.

Step 3. Provide coaching in parenting skills, the most important of which are parental expectancies of the child's behaviors, and the quantity and quality of communications between parent and child.

Step 4. Help parents define their values. Find out how they make decisions and how they understand the results of their actions toward their children. Role play and practice new parenting skills in structured situations with human service professionals. Work at home with new parenting skills, under skilled observation.

Step 5. Practice positive parenting skills under stress and in times of crisis. Old behaviors die hard, and reversion to old practices may occur initially during stress. A relapse is not critical, if the parent can figure out why the relapse occurred and offer corrective solutions.

Step 6. It is important that parents understand that long-term use of new skills depends upon attitudes. And as attitudes change, then so do the values that decide those attitudes.

SUMMARY

Of all life's pains, neglect and emotional mistreatment must be the cruelest. Yet it is difficult to call to the attention of our society and to hard to correct. We show disdain for physical abuse. We despise and hold in contempt sexual abuse. And with increasing sensitivity we discern verbal abuse. What then of emotional neglect? Perhaps we, as a social order, remain detached from something that we cannot legislate, cannot shape within the heart of another. And yet, the contents of the human heart are sensitive to change. Kindness and understanding produce kindness and understanding.

The issue may not be as complex as it appears. The solution may be that children, all children, need to be examined periodically in terms of their psychosocial growth. This may be is just as crucial as a physical health examination. As children grow, so shall they be.

THE FAMILY IN CRISIS

Dr. Kay Porter

"So?" he said, shrugging his shoulders. With "that look" on his face he turned and shut the door to his room. I lost control! Yanking his door open so forcefully it banged back loudly against the wall, I began to beat him on the back with both fists, screaming, "Don't you walk away from me, young man. I've had it with you! Do you hear? I've had it with you!" I continued to hit him. Driven by my anger, I couldn't stop. He moved quickly out of my range and sat down on his bed, his head lowered, his eyes downcast, quiet. Angry and breathless I left his room.

That was seven years ago. My son is now 24, but I can still see him sitting there. He's never mentioned it. I haven't either. I had promised myself I'd never do that to my kids. I'd treat him differently from the way my parents punished me. Each time I would say "Never again." But I did it again and again.

Her eyes filled with tears. The unresolved hurt showed on her face as she shared her "secret" with me.

Child abuse issues—emotional, physical, and sexual—face us daily on TV, in the newspapers, and in current popular magazines and professional journals. Awareness and thus concern about the way we treat our children is growing. Abuse has become an emotional issue that tears at the very heart of our families.

Difficult questions arise: Does abuse exist only in certain types of families, such as single-parent homes? Low-income families? Only among certain ethnic groups? Is child abuse more prevalent today than ever before? Who is to blame for abuse? What happens to the family unit in the midst of domestic violence? What can be done to help the family develop appropriate disciplinary practices?

We now know that child abuse occurs in a cross section of family types and across all socioeconomic lines—in wealthy homes and low-income homes, in families where both parents reside and in single-parent homes. The linking factors are the inability of the parents to change their abusive behaviors, and the powerlessness of their children to stop it.

CHANGING FAMILIES

The stability of the traditional American family and its values has been shaken. The rising divorce rate; increasing reports of child abuse; greater numbers of adolescents becoming involved with drugs, crime, and premarital pregnancy; accounts of violence between spouses—all point to this conclusion.

Many of us feel we need to get back to the strong family values of the past. And yet, that may be too simplistic an answer for such a complex issue. It is easy to draw the conclusion that today's family life is in serious trouble. Yet, a closer look at current trends shows us a different point of view. The family *is* alive in America today: it is simply taking on a new look.

Alternative family structures are slowly replacing our stereotypical nuclear family—the wage-earning father, dependent mother, and two or more children. However, the hallmark features of the functional family remain: its power, stability, and tolerance of change in response to the demands of the greater social structure. As America has changed, so has the family adjusted to the social flux, resulting in a variety of family forms.

The Family in Transition: From Farm to City

In the late 1800s most families worked together on the farm. Each family member had a given set of chores to complete. Although there was a vast difference in the type of work that each family member did, there was no distinction between the quantity of work done by men and women, or the value placed on that work. Each contribution was essential to the survival of the family. There was very little time for play and very little social life.

As our society became less agrarian and more industrialized, men began to work outside the home in factories and many families moved to the cities. The proportion of the population living in the cities radically increased; the days of the agrarian society had disappeared for all but a few.

Within city families, the husband became the sole breadwinner, while his wife ran the home and cared for the children. The fact that his wife and children were economically dependent upon the man's wage-earning ability elevated him to a position of greater value in the home. The distinction between the values placed on men's and women's work roles and the worth of all family members thus widened considerably.

Another consequence of this urbanization of the family was that the extended family, which had functioned as an important support system, was uprooted and separated. Friends from neighboring farms and the small-town community were no longer there to help in times of crisis. In the cities, families were on their own and had no one to depend upon but themselves. When they could not meet their needs, they turned to public and private agencies.

The Changing Status of Women

At the beginning of World War II women were needed as workers in the factories and elsewhere to replace their "soldier men." Women joined the work force in increasing numbers. Although some women remained in their nontraditional jobs after the war, most returned to their homemaker status as returning veterans reclaimed their jobs. Life returned to normal—the women remained in the home and the men resumed their roles as wage earners. During this period, society experienced its highest divorce rate up to that time.

In the late forties and fifties the United States experienced a postwar boom. Consumerism took hold. New household appliances and improved cars were available. New houses sprang up. During the fifties, sixties, and seventies a reverse movement took place: away from the cities, out to the suburbs. The American dream had been born: a larger house, two cars for each family, and many modern gadgets for the home. This was a very different standard of living from the farmhouse of yesterday.

It soon became apparent that one wage earner was not sufficient to meet the rising costs of the more affluent lifestyle of growing families and attractive consumer goods. Women began to seek jobs, usually in those positions typically thought of as "female"——nurses, secretaries, teachers, and so on. Young children were left with babysitters, placed in day-care centers, and attended preschool while both parents went off to work.

Recessions and increased automation in the period from 1950 to 1970 left many men unemployed. In some families, women became the primary wage earner. The number of working women greatly increased as they supplemented or replaced family income. This alteration in traditional role relationships often created multiple stressors, starting with the husband losing his job. When he became the househusband while his wife successfully entered the labor market, there was an additional stress. His role as full-time parent also may have led to other stressors.

With the number of divorces increasing each year, the number of single-parent families also rose. Most of these single heads of the household were mothers who needed to work to support their families. Even when adequate child support was forthcoming (which was not always the case), expenses far exceeded income. Again, children were without either parent during the day. Children of school age often came home to an empty house.

Hence the term "latchkey kids"——children who wear the key to their house on a cord around their neck to let themselves into their home each afternoon. Do you remember coming home from school calling: "Mom, I'm home"? Do you remember how important it was to you that she be there, and what an empty, let-down feeling it was when Mom wasn't home? These children lack attention and supervision every day for two to three hours. Often this absence of responsibility begins in the first and second grades.

The Impact of the Women's Movement

During the seventies and eighties the women's movement had considerable impact on the workplace. Women began to be employed in positions that, until that time, had been held mostly by men. Many of these women were successful and career-oriented. A new priority, in keeping with the new cry for self-satisfaction, occurred.

The seventies were a period of intense emotional introspection, in which the psychological well-being of self became a first concern. New self-help books pushed the idea that "I must work on me—you attend to your own problems." True to the seventies label, "the Me Decade," self-indulgence spread across the country with the directive, "If it feels good, do it." Meeting individual emotional and expressive needs was promoted, at least initially, at the sacrifice of the "we" in relationships.

The family suffered from the additional work-related stress of both parents' involvement in demanding jobs. Mother was absent from the home for longer periods, and when she returned, the job—not her family—was on her mind. Or, her fatigue made it difficult for her to attend to family problems. The stress and pressure from the workplace now entered the home through both parents. Children were too often seen as just another responsibility. The result was a further weakening of the home structure.

The Myth of the Ideal Marriage

In the fifties there had been an increased emphasis on companionship in marriage and the meeting of individual and emotional needs.[1] The nuclear family had become idealized. Within this ideal image, the mother's place was in the home, ministering to the personal and psychological needs of her husband and children.

The increased numbers of women in the workplace brought on a new set of problems for families.[2] With the emergence of the two-worker family, the position of women began to change. Since they were contributing to the higher financial status of the family, women began to expect a larger role in economic and other decisions.

The question has been raised, "How do the demands for more equality in marital power affect the stability of marriage?"[3] Some researchers argue that equality is synonymous with a move toward individualism, which will further undermine the value of the family. Others maintain that more gender equality will result in more satisfaction within the marriage. Still others argue that more equality will benefit the children through improved quality of parenting.

A further development in the evolution of the family was the increased availability of birth-control measures, which gave women new freedom to experience sex outside marriage.[4] Women's ability to control whether they would become pregnant led to a sexual revolution, primarily experienced by the ability to participate in sex as recreation. Some women even chose to have children without the benefit of marriage.

These changes affected both the function of and attitude toward marriage.[5] Without the need for the so-called protective and fulfilling advantages of marriage, women could feel freer to get out of a marriage that did not meet their emotional needs.

New Family Structures

Our view of the traditional nuclear family has changed in response to the many alternative family forms springing up in the sixties, seventies, and eighties.

Despite the rising number of divorces since the beginning of this century, there is little evidence to suggest that this reflects disillusionment with marriage or family life. In fact, the trend is reversing. In the July 19, 1990 issue of *USA Today* a report from the National Center for Health Statistics stated that the divorce rate was down from 5.2 (per 1,000 people) in 1980 to 4.7 in 1989.

Current research shows a pattern of "serial monogamy" emerging. Thus the divorce-and-remarriage cycle causes "blended" families. These families often consist of a previously married spouse, children from a previous marriage, and children from the new marriage.

More people live together without getting married: unwed couples, homosexual couples, and communal living couples, for instance. There are also mothers who choose to have children but not husbands, and the number of children being born to unwed teenagers is increasing.

Also, the number of single-parent families is rapidly increasing. Single-parent families are not of necessity pathological, although the terms used to describe them—"father-absent families" and "broken homes"—tend to foster the idea.

Divorce often leaves a woman with (1) young children, (2) financial problems, and (3) a limited social/family support system. Without the necessary support system these families can experience tremendous stress and difficulty. The single parent, be it father or mother, has a tough road ahead.

These various lifestyles need not be inherently bad. The trends in today's family do not, in and of themselves, ensure weak relationships or develop into unhealthy modes of communication. Nor do they necessarily create abusing families. Dysfunctional patterns of interaction can surface in all types of families. The system of rules, values, and beliefs that family members live by influences their behaviors and shapes the kind of adults the children will become.

Alternative family lifestyles do point, however, to a decline in the importance of the traditional nuclear family structure. They show how experiencing added stress and tension can easily create dysfunctional patterns of interaction among family members. It is important to re-emphasize that these dysfunctional ways of relating can surface in all types of families.

THE EFFECTS OF DIVORCE

"I should never have had kids. I wish you'd never been born. You're just like your father—bad clear through." My mother's words reverberated in my ears as she walked angrily upstairs and shut herself up in her bedroom. I could hear her crying. Then she came downstairs, got in the car and drove off. I was afraid. Was she gone for good? Was she ever coming back? I began to cry. I was three years old the first time it happened. That was right after THE DIVORCE! Those words were said often. Each time I wished something could be different. I wished I had never been born either! Somewhere along the line

I decided I didn't want to be that kind of mother . . . but I am.

All too often people marry to solve problems; to shield themselves from becoming individuals. Too often, people marry to their weaknesses. We bring to the marriage "the family of our youth" inside us. We tend to seek out those who relate to us as did our parents—both the good and the bad, healthy and unhealthy.[6]

We bring to the marriage yesterday's unresolved conflicts.[7] Today's conflicts can build on, or stem from, yesterday's, and the inability to deal with these conflicts creates dysfunctional patterns of relating. Without resolution, divorce often results.

Research on the effects of divorce shows that it produces patterns of development that are not only *different* but also *disturbed*.[8] The incidence of second divorces shows that outward signs of stability may mask unresolved issues.[9] Clearly, if an individual does not grow beyond his or her weaknesses, beyond the unhealthy areas of personality, a next relationship or marriage also may produce life problems. The high divorce rate among second and third marriages attests to this.[10]

One does not need to search for the hurt, devastation, or psychological maladjustment of divorce; it is there for everyone to view. The pain of divorce leaves no one in the family untouched. Judith Wallerstein, in a follow-up study called *Children of Divorce*, found that many young people, even ten years after their parents' divorce, still spoke sorrowfully about their emotional deprivation. They still carried with them unresolved conflicts.[11] Following are some quotes from the Wallerstein study:

Larry remembered plates being broken, both of his parents sitting on the bed crying, and his father leaving in a sports car.

Robert said that he remembered nothing. All he remembers is that he didn't understand what was going on, and he didn't really know whether he was supposed to have two parents.

Linda said, 'The hardest thing for me is that through the years there has been no one there for me.'

Dierdre said, 'I worry about mom sometimes. I want her to be happy. Sometimes she is sad and depressed and I feel sad.'

Lindsay said that it was great that her mother had done so well in her own career, but she added, 'Most of my problem is during the day when mom is away. Maybe if mom was home I wouldn't be in so much trouble. It was an empty house and an empty feeling that got me into sex and drugs.'

Linda said, 'If I had kids it would be real hard to get a divorce. Divorce isn't easy on kids.' Linda, too, confessed how frightened she was about repeating her mother's mistake. 'I worry that it will be the same for me. People get blinded and run off and it doesn't work, and then they're left with nothing. I worry very much that I won't pick the right guy, that it will be somebody who is abusive. It's real likely.'

Wallerstein concluded that, for many children in the study—close to thirty percent—the divorce remained a powerful memory, eliciting strong feelings even ten years after the break-up. She maintains that divorce adversely affects children of all ages. Those who were youngest at the time of the marital breakup fare better in the following years than their older siblings. Divorce creates a crisis in the family life cycle—a state of imbalance experienced by all members of the nuclear and extended family.

Recent census bureau figures show that nearly one-fourth of children under eighteen today live with only one parent. Ninety percent of the time a female functions as the head of the household. Some researchers estimate that nearly half today's children will experience the divorce of their parents. Incidents of divorce have tripled in the past three decades, with 1.2 million divorces reported in 1982.

Although I believe divorce should be a very last alternative, I realize there are situations where to remain in the marriage would be more damaging than to divorce. Simply the stopping of marital conflict provides a badly needed healing. In these instances, the divorce process results in both grief and growth.

If, however, divorce is so traumatic, so harmful to all involved, why not work harder to prevent it? Why not work harder to strengthen the commitment to the relationship? Why not go into marriage better equipped with healthy methods of relating?

HOW DYSFUNCTIONAL FAMILIES EVOLVE

The family can and should be a haven from the harshness and confusion of the outside world. Sadly, this is not so for many.

Once it was believed that if one could only solve personal problems, relationships would take care of themselves. If two people love each other, says the ideal, that is enough to ensure success in marriage. Despite this belief, happiness often eludes us, especially at home. We struggle against the anxiety we feel. We long for freedom. If only we didn't need others! If only others didn't need and depend on us—then we would be free! But here is the paradox: As long as we fail to recognize our connection to others, we can never be free to be ourselves.[12]

Most of us honestly try to improve our marriages, relate better with our children, and respond in healthy ways to our parents. When this fails we become discouraged and turn to other sources for contentment and satisfaction. We look for ways to find a "fix"—alcohol, eating, spending, affairs, TV, hobbies. Addictive behavior develops. Dysfunctional patterns of interaction become habitual, and anger and frustration mount. Often those who experience our anger and frustration most harshly are the ones we are closest to—family members.

Soon, as the needs of individuals in the family go unmet, no one can discuss it. Communication becomes more difficult. Family members begin to enforce unspoken rules, and harsh treatment follows. Abusive behavior becomes part of family interaction.

Characteristics of Abusive Parents

People need completion because their own needs have not been not met, and their needs were not met because their parents were not there for them. Many people marry to rid themselves of this feeling of incompleteness. They are willing to give to another to receive in return what will make them whole. They give to get a counterfeit form of love. Eventually, consciously or unconsciously, they begin to feel that having a child will meet this need.

There has been much discussion regarding personality characteristics that abusive parents have in common.[13] Although little agreement has emerged among the attempts to construct such a portrait, three characteristics stand out:

1. an acceptance of abuse as a parent's way of life;
2. a tendency to harbor grossly unrealistic expectations of children or to view them as evil; and
3. a background of abuse in their own childhood.

Guilt and Shame

All needs can be shamed in a dysfunctional family. The children will be shamed through abandonment, and ultimately they will internalize the shame just as their parents did.

Marilyn Mason, in her book, *Facing Shame*, gives this definition of shame:

> . . . *humiliation so painful, embarrassment so deep, and a sense of being so completely diminished that one feels he or she will disappear into a pile of ashes. A pervasive sense of shame is the ongoing premise that one is bad, defective, or unworthy. While guilt is a painful feeling of regret and responsibility for one's actions, shame is a painful feeling about oneself as a person.*[14]

Bradshaw, in *The Family*, says: "Guilt says I've done something wrong; shame says there is something wrong with me."[15]

The distinction between guilt and shame is important. Guilt does not reflect directly upon one's identity nor diminish one's sense of personal worth. It comes from the violation of one or more of an internalized set of values. It can teach or reinforce limits.

Shame, on the other hand, does not allow one to learn from mistakes. It only reinforces negative feelings about oneself, and internalizes the message that one is unlovable or unworthy.

The roots of shame come from abuse and personal violations that destroy boundaries, trampling upon the children's need for security. Because security is not present on the inside, children constantly seek security and attachment outside. This can lead to their willingness to continue being misused and abused.

Most of us can readily admit that physical or sexual abuse causes damage to the abused child. It is not difficult to recognize this sort of abuse when we see it, and we ache for the child who lives with such a situation. But it is the subtle, insidious form of abuse so current today in dysfunctional families that I wish to address here: the emotional abuse that produces shame.

Family Rules and the Creation of Shame

Families are dynamic social systems having structure and rules. Those family rules reveal parents' beliefs about raising children. Indeed, they tell children what it means to be a human being.

Religious teaching and the schools often reinforce family rules: "Honor your father and mother"; "Honesty is the best policy." Some of these rules, handed down from grandparents to parents to children, can become toxic: "Children should be seen and not heard." "Children should always obey adults (all adults)." One rule many homes embrace is that the rules should never be questioned— this would dishonor parents! A rule often forgotten is the

Golden Rule: "Treat others as you would like to be treated."

Eight Rules that Create Dysfunction

There are eight unspoken family rules that foster a "shame-bound" system.[16] Operating unconsciously to create distress in the family, these eight covert rules represent a recurrent emerging pattern. All eight rules may not be present in each family.

1. **Control**: Be in control of behavior and interactions. Control is a major defensive strategy. It gives a sense of power, although it is motivated not so much by a drive for power as by a drive for predictability and security. In a family, one or more family members rigidly hold this control and power over the others. Those without power live in anxious fear of those who have it.

2. **Perfectionism**: Always be "right" in everything you do. The family that emphasizes this rule is intelligent, high achieving, and well dressed; "winners" in all external ways. They are constantly comparing themselves to an external norm, trying to measure up. No rule leads to hopelessness faster than this one, because the ideal doesn't allow for mistakes.

3. **Blame**: If something doesn't happen as you planned, blame someone (yourself or others). Blame is a defensive cover-up for shame. "If it weren't for you, I'd be happy." Self-blame is a direct expression of this rule. Though self-blame is painful, it allows the blame to remain in charge of interactions and reduces surprise or spontaneity.

4. **Denial:** Deny feelings, especially the negative or vulnerable ones like anxiety, fear, loneliness, grief, rejection, and need. Family members function well in less intimate relationships at work and school.

5. **Unreliability:** Don't expect reliability in relationships. Don't trust anyone and you won't be disappointed.

6. **Incompleteness:** Don't bring transactions to completion or resolution. Disagreements can go unresolved for years. The family can insist on maintaining tranquility, and no open disagreement takes place. They don't face the problems, so the problems never get solved. Or, the opposite may occur: constant chronic fidgeting with no resolution.

7. **No-talk:** Don't talk openly about feelings, thoughts, or experiences that focus on the pain and loneliness or the lack of healthy functioning. This rule operates in sexual abuse families where people never verbalize their suspicions; they know what is happening but they never tell anyone.

8. **Myth-making:** Always look on the bright side. Reframe or disguise the hurt, pain, and distress to distract others from knowing what is really going on. This rule preserves the status quo.

Parents parent themselves with these rules. Without honestly looking at them or updating them, parents pass them on to their children. The rules play themselves inside, repeatedly, as if on a tape recorder.

Shame and the Creation of Ego Defenses

In her book *Facing Shame*, Marilyn Mason states: "A shame-bound family is a family with a self-sustaining, multigenerational system of interaction with a cast of characters who are loyal to a set of rules and who demand control and perfectionism and practice blame and denial. The pattern inhibits or defeats the development of authentic intimate relationships, promotes secrets and vague personal boundaries, unconsciously instills shame in the family members and chaos in their lives, and binds them to perpetuate the shame in themselves and their kin. It does so despite the good intentions, wishes, and love that also may be part of the system."[17]

Shame prevents intimacy, since each family member is afraid to let the others know their own fright or hurt.[18] Family members don't show or share their feelings. Holding on to their secrets, not feeling good about themselves, most people in shame feel isolated and lonely.

Children have a great need to belong, to be a part of another, to have an attachment to another. They strive to learn the rules Mom and Dad set down for the family, to please them. They attempt to follow rigid standards of perfectionism. They may say to themselves, "If only I were smarter, or better looking; If only I got along better at school; If only . . .; then all would be fine." It is all but impossible to feel good about ourself when we are always being measured by someone else's yardstick! It's difficult to live up to expectations that always seem just beyond our reach. For some, attempting to be a part of the family, remaining loyal to parents, must occur at great sacrifice to self. Children become victims in troubled families. Children who grow up in a troubled family, with all its dysfunctional rules, are destined to suffer from feelings of loneliness, anger, hurt, guilt, and shame. They learn to live with the constant fear of rejection, punishment, or abandonment.

It is at this point that the ego defenses come into play. The child creates an illusion of loving, caring parents, denying what is going on. Anger is displaced onto self or others, feelings repressed. The child even dissociates so the hurt and horror cannot be felt or experienced.

Children in a dysfunctional family survive by learning how to respond to the stress or abuse in the family with behaviors such as denial, repression, dissociation, withdrawal, or anger. As children grow up, these "survival behaviors" continue although the children no longer are exposed to the original source of stress. These behaviors feel normal, because they were needed for survival every day in their childhood. In adulthood, these patterns are no longer needed, and so they become unhealthy coping responses.

WHO ARE THEY? WHO AM I?

It is from families, healthy or unhealthy, that children first learn who they are. They see themselves through the mirroring eyes of their parents. From parents children first learn about emotions and intimacy. Parents model for children, intentionally and unintentionally, what feelings are acceptable and what feelings are inappropriate or forbidden. Parents teach their children the meaning of the world around them. To neglect a child's basic needs, to fail to give affirmation, is a form of abandonment. No one is there for the child to depend on.

Just as parenting dictates children's beliefs about themselves, parenting also forms children's beliefs about parents. For the first years of a child's life, parents are the most important part of the child's world. Parents are the child's protectors. No harm can befall the child as long as the parents are there. The magical thinking of a child makes parents all-powerful and God-like.

Even if parents hurt or neglect their children, abusing them emotionally or physically, children will accept the blame and assume they deserved such treatment. These children will assume they are bad to maintain the God-like image of their parents and to keep their protectors. No child wants to believe parents are wrong or imperfect.

Let us repeat that emphatically: Children want to believe parents are right or perfect. Therefore, children believe they are responsible in some way for the way their parents act, and when "bad" things occur it must be the children's fault. This makes them innately bad. They believe there is something profoundly wrong with who they are. Shame begets shame.

A shame-bound family is a group of people, all of whom feel alone together.

CONFUSING PUNISHMENT WITH TEACHING

"Why did you punish your daughter so severely?" Her father looked up, surprised at my question. "I just whipped her hard enough and long enough to make sure she'd never do that again. That's the way my father did it to me. She'll know better next time." His wife nodded in agreement as did their seven-year-old daughter, supporting his point of view. His daughter bore the marks and bruises as well as the emotional scars from the many whippings.

Parents given to child abuse seem to consider physical punishment as natural and appropriate for their children. Few of these parents distinguish between teaching and punishment. For these parents it is never too early to begin showing who is in charge. With these values and beliefs it is not surprising that the fine line between child discipline and child abuse often become blurred. These parents simply do not see corporal punishment as related to abuse; instead they are "doing what comes naturally"—which often means doing what their parents did to them.

As previously mentioned, a background of abuse in their own childhood often emerges as a commonality among parents who abuse their children physically or sexually.[19] It is from these neglected and violated children that the next generation of abusive parents will come. In *The Battered Child*, Brandt Steele says:

> *These unfortunate people have carried with them into adult life their main psychological patterns of lack of trust, fear of social contacts, inability to have pleasure, low self-esteem, mild depression, great neediness and inability to love empathically . . . . When they have children they repeat the behavior of their own parents; they expect their children to behave in ways to satisfy the excessive parental needs. Especially in times of crises the parents turn to their babies for comfort; the children are bound to fail and suffer punishment or neglect. The cycle repeats itself.*

This cycle reinforces the feelings of shame and abandonment. Often-abused children, because they see themselves as bad and experience the shame of feeling worthless, cling even more tenaciously to the belief that parents are totally good and always do what is right. These children are so needy they hold on to the family rules so as not to part with their idealized parents. All the while, however, the children sense the rejection and abandonment from their parents. Since parents are the ones who initially meet children's needs, the abused children go wanting. The emptiness remains, denial continues, and shame becomes a constant companion. Bradshaw calls this "the cup with a hole in it."

Children with these internalized feelings then become adults. As adults they cast about to find someone to supply the love and acceptance they never received from their parents. They seek out another dysfunctional adult—who may be as emotionally unavailable as were their parents—to fill the cup. They create a dysfunctional marriage, which in turn creates a dysfunctional family. The shame remains. History repeats itself. This family carries a multi-generational sense of shame—a wound acted upon day after day, generation after generation. As long as families leave conflicts unresolved, the vulnerability exists to repeat similar patterns in new relationships.

REVERSING THE CYCLE OF ABUSE

The group had just begun. A young mother, a social worker employed by the local university, spoke up. "It's frightening," she said. "About two years ago I was so full of rage, so filled with anger that I wanted to lash out at my kids. I could have really hurt them. At times I wanted to. It was very frightening knowing how close I came.

A professor once told our class: "The difference between parents who abuse their children and those who don't is the ones who do abuse their children, abuse them." Read that again. Yes, almost all parents have felt pushed to the point of frustration and have experienced the wild feeling of striking out at those they love. We have come close to that fine line.

What is a healthy family? How does a dysfunctional family rid itself of the hurt and shame embodied in its members? How do they change the behaviors that would entrap them? How do they create a new set of rules? How do they set aside those survival behaviors that no longer serve them well?

Families can travel the road to health, but usually they must seek help. Only with much effort can they break the damaging cycle of shame and abuse. A therapist can guide individuals and families to a better understanding of themselves and each other.

It is not an easy road. Awareness of what is happening is the first step. Healing and changing take time. Parents must first resolve their conflicts and meet their needs with each other; children should not be used to provide the parents with a sense of power and worth. Unresolved conflict with one's own family of origin also makes it difficult to move forward with a new family. These issues need to be looked at and dealt with accordingly.

An awareness of one's own feelings and a sense of self-worth and self-trust must be developed. Each must regain —if he or she ever had it—the dependence on self and faith in one's own capacity to cope with the environment, with people, with thoughts and emotions.

A good relationship, between parents or between parents and children, is based on unconditional love and acceptance. Self-worth comes from such support. Each knows the other has made the commitment to stand by, to be there, committed, no matter what. The home becomes a haven from the world.

RATIONAL DISCIPLINE

Dr. Robert R. Smith

When parents discipline impulsively, out of anger, physical or verbal abuse often occurs. Rational discipline, in contrast, is training that develops self-control, character, orderliness, and efficiency. When anger is present none of these are taught. Other extreme emotions, such as depression, anxiety, and fear, also interfere with teaching children.

Much emotional upset can be self-controlled. This does not mean that the more serious problems of life can all be dealt with simply and that outside therapy may not be helpful or required. Simple self-control techniques can be taught, and with practice learned, once individuals understand how thoughts create emotions that, in turn, lead to behaviors. A brief overview of cognitive psychology helps to provide a better understanding of this.

COGNITIVE PSYCHOLOGY AND SELF-CONTROL

Cognitive psychology, or the study of memory, perception, problem-solving, and language- and information-processing, originated in the nineteenth century. Central to the theory of emotional upset, according to cognitive psychologists, was the idea that emotional disturbance is influenced by maladaptive or irrational beliefs and thoughts. The individual's emotional upset results from distortions of reality based on false premises and assumptions.

Helping people, from this perspective, includes unraveling distorted thinking (not feelings) and teaching them how to think more realistically. Common distortions or errors in thought processes of angry or depressed individuals include:

1. *arbitrary inference* (drawing a conclusion based on missing or false evidence);
2. *overgeneralization* (a simple instance applies to an entire cluster or phenomenon);
3. *magnification or exaggeration*, selective abstraction (disregard for an important element in a situation);
4. personalization (individuals relate an external circumstance to themselves when there is no basis for this relationship);
5. *dichotomous reasoning* (allowing only two possible evaluations of an event: right or wrong, good or bad, or success or failure); and
6. *oversocialization* (failure to appreciate the arbitrariness of many cultural mores).

Albert Ellis and Maxie Maultsby are two of the best known cognitive theorists and therapists.[1] In their early clinical work, both found that although classical psychotherapy helped individuals find insight, it did little to help individuals deal more effectively with their problems. Their new approach borrowed from the stoic philosopher,

Epictetus, who said that it is not facts or events that upset man but the view he takes of them.

Maultsby and Ellis developed their own people-helping, self-help approaches. Maultsby's *Rational Behavior Therapy* (RBT) and Ellis' *Rational Emotive Therapy* (RET) have been helping individuals overcome emotional upset for several decades. The focus of this chapter will be on how to apply Rational Behavior Therapy to yourself. With work and practice, people begin to see that a self-help, therapeutic approach allows them to deal more effectively with the irritations and disappointments of life.

Rational Behavior Therapy (RBT)

Maultsby's RBT began with Ellis's observations. Ellis believed that people are biologically and culturally predisposed to choose, create, relate, and enjoy. But they are just as predisposed to conform, to be suggestible, to hate, and to arbitrarily block their enjoyment. Although people have a remarkable capacity to observe, reason, and enhance their experience, they also have a tendency to ignore reality and misuse reason. They rigidly invent demons that sabotage their health and happiness. When people refuse to accept reality, they create their own emotional disturbance.

To Ellis and Maultsby, acting-out behavior associated with emotional disturbance is a manifestation of three human tendencies: (1) although people deny that they believe in magic, they act as if they do believe in it; (2) without realizing it, people often mix inappropriate past memories with present reality; and (3) people prefer long-standing patterns of repetitive behavior to new adaptive learning or problem-solving abilities. Maultsby pioneered in adapting Ellis's understanding and treating of emotional disturbance to the self-counseling area. Understanding how the human brain works is important in understanding how clients can help themselves to better deal with emotional upsets.

How the Brain Juggles Thoughts and Feelings. As described by Maultsby, the brain allows us to perceive. It creates images of our perceptions and combines the stored images with our beliefs. Behavior then follows. Two main parts of the brain that control emotional and physical behavior are the neocortex and the limbic system, the thinking and feeling parts, respectively. Nerves link the neocortex and limbic system with each other and with the sense organs. The sense organs—eyes, ears, skin, for example—allow the neocortex and limbic system to notice and react to the world, but not always rationally.

Thoughts in the neocortex can be typed as positive, negative, neutral, or as a combination of these. Thoughts cause feelings that, in turn, cause behavior. For example, if a father perceives an event as horrible or awful, such as failing to get his child to behave as he wishes, then feelings of anger or perhaps self-depreciation emerge. This leads to ineffective parenting: yelling and screaming at the child, hitting, or ignoring the child's behavior. He does not see how best to handle the situation. Instead, his ineffective behaviors stem from revenge or self-incrimination.

Eleven Irrational Beliefs

An essential idea of *Rational Emotive Therapy* is the falseness of certain beliefs that many parents usually accept as true, like: "I must be a perfect parent" or "Children (people) should do what I want them to do." When we continuously repeat these beliefs to ourselves, we not only accept, but also strengthen, them. These beliefs form the basis of emotional upset, because no human being is perfect and not everyone does what other people want them to do.

There are eleven major irrational beliefs:[2]

1. It is essential to be loved or approved of by almost everyone in the community (e.g., My children—others—must respect me).
2. One must be absolutely competent, adequate, and achieving to consider oneself worthwhile (e.g., I must be a perfect parent/friend).
3. Some people are bad, wicked or villainous and, therefore, should be blamed and punished (e.g., Errant children—others—must be punished for their bad deeds).
4. It is a catastrophe when things are not as I want them to be (e.g., It's awful when children—others—do not do what I want them to do).
5. Unhappiness is caused by outside circumstances and the individual has no control over it (e.g., These children—people—make me upset).
6. Dangerous or fearsome things are causes for great concern, and their possibilities must be continually dwelt upon (e.g., Bringing up children is frightening; I'll never be able to do it right).
7. It is easier to avoid certain difficulties and self-responsibilities than to face them (e.g., I'll let the school discipline my child because I'm unable).
8. One should be dependent on others and must have someone stronger on whom to rely (e.g., My husband/wife will do most of the child rearing).

9. Past events and experiences are the determinants of present behavior; the influence of the past cannot be eradicated (e.g., I'm a real hothead and I'll never change).
10. One should be very upset over other people's problems and disturbances (e.g., I'm just devastated that my child has acne/didn't make the cheerleading squad).
11. There is always a right or perfect solution to every problem, and it must be found or the results will be catastrophic (e.g., My children must be good and I must find a way to make them be).

When parents believe these irrational ideas, they exaggerate life's unpleasant but inevitable events, such as children not doing what parents want them to. In response, they command or demand that the children change.

Ellis refers to this as "absolutistic" thinking. We perceive the event as a catastrophe, the worst thing that could happen, comparable to, for instance, losing a loved one to death or a house to fire. It is black or white and never grey. "I must be a perfect parent, a perfect person, and have my children always do what I want them to do."

Parents need to understand first that people are not perfect, they can never be perfect, and the world does not operate in a precise way. An easy way to remember this idea is to examine three words that parents need to define and better understand. These words, coupled with beliefs like "I must be perfect," will always lead to disaster. The three words are *awful*, *should*, and *can't stand*. Parents who examine the true meaning of these words will begin to understand how the words themselves help to create emotional upset.

Consider the word "awful" or any one of the hundreds of synonyms such as "horrible," "terrible," or "rotten to the core." "Awful" turns a normal setback or disappointment in life, like not getting children to do what you want, into an end-of-the-world disaster. Not getting a child to do something is definitely a disappointment, but it is not a disaster.

Words like "should," "ought," "must," and "have to" turn desires into demands. I "must" have a perfect child or things "should" or "must" go my way; if these do not happen, I am going to be upset. Things do not *have* to go our way. It would be nice, but it does not have to be any other way than the way it is. "Can't stand" is a phrase that turns frustrations into impossibilities. Life is often frustrating, even unfair. Children, occasionally, do not or will not do what one wants them to do. This is to be expected.

It is how parents handle these kinds of frustrations that will set the conditions for the outcome. Handling relationships with children calmly and positively, not out of anger, is the best possible way to enhance parenting skills and teach effective discipline. By keeping a cool head, parents will be less inclined to scream, yell, or strike out in other ways. Parents will feel something, but it will not be outrage. It will only be annoyance. When enraged anger is not present, parents can think more clearly of ways to handle the problem constructively.

The ABC Model

The "ABC" model is an effective way of viewing reactions. Therapists take active roles in teaching clients the ABC model during Rational Behavior Therapy. Methods of teaching will vary with therapists.

At *point A* (activating event) upsetting stimuli occur; for example, a daughter refuses to clean up her room. The ideal is for the parent to view the event objectively. An objective parent concludes, at *point B* (rational belief), that this is unfortunate and that a change needs to occur to make the event less irritating at *point C* (consequence) where the parent feels annoyance.

However, not tolerating a child's refusal to clean up her room at point B (now called an irrational belief) exaggerates the situation. The event thus becomes "awful," "horrible," and "catastrophic," the worst thing in the world. The parent now feels the consequence (point C) of rage, instead of irritation. Inappropriate feelings interfere with the parent doing something constructively about point A (the event), condemning the parent or child—or both—for being imperfect. The result is inappropriate parental behavior.

A cognitive therapist practicing rational behavior therapy shows parents how their past and present illogical thinking is creating their problems by:

1. bringing such thinking to their attention;
2. reviewing how they are causing and maintaining their disturbance and unhappiness;
3. showing exactly what the illogical links are; and
4. teaching them how to rethink, challenge, contradict, and reverbalize such links so that their internalized thoughts of perfection and need for respect from others, specifically their children, become more rational.

Rational Self-Analysis (RSA)

Now parents can begin to practice a simple but workable method of Rational Behavior Therapy, the Rational Self-Analysis (RSA). Parents should practice the Rational Self-Analysis by writing it out at least twice a day for several weeks so that they gain confidence in the approach.

Practicing Rational Self-Analysis is like a football player memorizing plays. If we ask a football player what "R32 right" means before training camp, he would not able to explain the play. By the opening game, however, when the quarterback shouts "R32 right!" first to the left, then to the right, and then, "hut hut!," the well-practiced team moves off the ball like a machine. How did the team get to be a well-oiled machine for the play "R32 right"? They spent many hours practicing that and many other plays. The quarterback had only to cue the team members, and the rest was automatic.

All that parents have to remember is the self-analysis cue "RSA" when they are confronted by an unpleasant, anger-provoking, potentially depressing situation. The RSA cues parents to take action in their brain. They need to rethink and reevaluate the event, and remember what happens when they think irrational thoughts.

The following is an example of a typical self-analysis procedure with a parent, the "great expecter."

Event or Happening. (Write down what happened; not what you think or feel about it, but just a description of the event.)

Your daughter refused to clean her room after you asked her nicely to do it quickly. She said she was not going to do it this minute.

Self-Talk or Opinion: Write down what you said to yourself. Think of the "awfuls," "shoulds," and "can't stands" and the eleven irrational ideas.

1. *She should not refuse to do what I want her to do.*
2. *It's awful that she does not mind me.*
3. *I can't stand not getting respect from her. (There may always be other self-talk.)*

Emotions and Actions: Write down how you felt and what you did.

Anger. Screamed and yelled that she had better clean the room now or else!

Rational Challenges. Go back to B. Take each self-talk statement, one at a time (there may be only one or more than three). Ask yourself why you tell yourself "shoulds," "awfuls," or "can't stands." Reason out each of these. In other words, prove to yourself that it was not a should, an awful, or a can't stand. Once you have proven that the statement was not a "should" but a "wish"; or an "irritation" instead of an end-of-the-world disaster "awful"; or a "frustration" rather than an impossible "can't stand," write a more rational statement for each in this section.

1. *She does not have to do everything I want her to do. My should is a demand that came from my wish. It would have been better if I thought of it as a desire or wish rather than a command or demand.*
2. *It's not an awful, end-of-the-world disaster like our house burning down; it is only irritating or annoying. I can prove that to myself.*

3. *I can stand not getting respect from my daughter. How do I know that? Because I am standing it. I may not be very happy, or like it, but I am standing it. To not stand something means that you would have to die. So her refusal, although I am not happy about it, did not kill me. It's not impossible.*

New Feelings: Write in new feelings that probably would come from thinking the thoughts in section D.

Annoyance or irritation, perhaps disappointment or other less charged emotions.

New Thinking: Write in new problem-solving thinking here. If your feelings were less charged, like those above, you could think more clearly about how you might handle your daughter's refusal. You could think more effectively and come up with a better strategy. Write in the new strategy.

New Behavior: Write in the proposed new behavior. Now you are ready to carry out your problem-solving strategy with your daughter. There are many possible approaches. One might be to ask her calmly to help you understand why she does not want to do it right now. Or, you might ask her if she could do it if you helped her. There are many other strategies that you will think of if you remain calm.

It's best to practice the RSA model away from the problem, alone in a quiet room. Parents should mentally rehearse the RSA frequently, going over each step, imagining what would happen if they did not challenge their irrational thoughts.[3] Practicing writing and imagining until they are as comfortable as football players in the "R32 right" example helps parents discipline their children more confidently and effectively.

SUMMARY

All healthy human brains function the same way. When unpleasant things happen, our self-talk creates our feelings. We act from those feelings. If our thoughts as parents are based on irrational ideas or beliefs like "Our children (others) should do what we want them to do because we must be respected by everyone and we must be perfect," our feeling will automatically be intense. The behavior coming from the charged feelings, like anger, will not be as effective as we would like. To correct those feelings, parents need to practice rational thinking. The Rational Self-Analysis helps them do that.

GETTING HELP
Dr. Robert R. Smith

Experts expect to see even more child abuse and neglect because the mental health of Americans will continue to decline into the twenty-first century. Current estimates place the number of people in the United States with mental health disorders at forty million, up from an estimated thirty-three million in 1980.[1] Mental health service needs are increasing because people live longer, there are more children being raised in single-parent households, and technology shifts cause relocations with periods of unemployment and financial distress.

While millions of individuals suffer from mental health disorders and will engage in child abuse and neglect, the system designed to help them is already overburdened, and will become even more so. There is another complication, too. As families have become more mobile and scattered and as communities have become more complex, so have our sources of information and help. While the treatment system as a whole is inadequate to meet the total need for services, there is also a fragmentation of services among many different private, volunteer, self-help and public agencies. Today, we expect parents to choose wisely among a wide array of sources in a community. But parents seeking help are confused.

Parents wonder to whom do they turn for advice about normal child behaviors for a specific developmental period, and what should their expectations be? Whom do they ask about the appropriateness their parental behavior, especially if it seems out of control? How does one find a *Parents Anonymous* group, and how does one know whether contact within this group provides confidential help rather than ridicule or even scandal? This chapter offers some practical advice to parents seeking help.

PREVENTION

While counseling and psychotherapy are effective, the current and future mental health demands call for rethinking and a reorientation toward prevention. The current and future human service delivery world is being shaped by a four basic assumptions:

1. People's environments may either limit or nurture them; for instance, when a child is victimized by a destructive family.
2. A multifaceted approach to helping is more efficient than a single-service approach; that is, group intervention rather than the more traditional one-to-one counseling/psychological approach.
3. Prevention is more efficient than remediation. The medical world, which, in many ways, has dominated the helping professions until recently, focused on "illness" and sought to cure in a doctor-patient, one-to-one model. Prevention, on the other hand, builds on the clients' strength and teaches life skills necessary for life management.

4. Community-counseling is adaptable to all human service delivery settings, such as schools, prisons,
hospitals, and corporations. A community is a system
of interdependent persons, groups, and organizations
that: (a) meet the individual's primary needs; (b)
affects the individual's daily life; and (c) mediates
between the individual and society.[2]

Are You Vulnerable?

If prevention continues to be a cornerstone in how human-
service delivery is being or will be shaped, how do professionals fit into the scheme? The answer is by emphasizing
primary prevention. This means deliberate psychological
education, similar to parent, death, and sex education.
Secondary prevention refers to crisis counseling, sex
therapy, and the like; an example of tertiary prevention is
supportive therapy. All three forms of prevention may be
needed in helping, but primary prevention is the focus.

Helping people recognize that they are vulnerable to
mental health problems is the first step in primary prevention. An interesting way to begin is for parents to complete Holmes and Rahe's ranked list of potentially stressful life events.[3] Are you experiencing or have you recently
experienced the following life events? The more of these
that you have experienced, the more vulnerable you are to
stress-related family problems such as child abuse.

Death of spouse
Divorce
Marital separation
Jail term
ı Death of close family member
ᵥ Personal injury or illness

Marriage
Fired from job
Marital reconciliation
Retirement
Change in health of family member
Pregnancy
Sex difficulties
Gain of new family member
Change in financial state
Death of close friend
Change to different line of work
Change in number of arguments with spouse
Mortgage over $10,000
Foreclosure of mortgage or loan
Change in responsibilities at work
Son or daughter leaving home
Trouble with in-laws
Outstanding personal achievement
Wife beginning or stopping work
Beginning or ending school
Revision of personal habits
Trouble with boss
Change in hours or work conditions
Change in residence
Change in schools
Change in recreation
Change in social activities
Mortgage or loan less than $10,000
Change in sleeping habits
Change in number of family get-togethers
Change in eating habits
Vacation
Minor violations of the law

Finding Help

After discussing your vulnerability to mental health problems, a counselor would help you work through available
resources to find the most appropriate help, protection, or
both. A sample list of resources available in a typical
community follows. This list is not exhaustive and would
vary among communities. There also would be some
overlap and repetition because of the fragmentation of the
human service delivery model I mentioned before. For
instance, Employee Assistance Programs provided by
major employers would use both selected private practitioners and mental health centers.

1. Close friends or relatives who are good listeners,
   who do not enable, and who know how to refer
   more serious problems
2. Pastoral counselors (ministers, priests, rabbis)
3. Employee Assistance Programs (EAPs)
4. Private practitioners (counselors, psychologists,
   social workers, or others)
5. Mental health centers/associations
6. Self-help mutual support groups
7. Domestic violence shelters/centers
8. Community referral services

Often colleges and public school systems provide short
courses or workshops on parenting skills and stress and
anger management techniques. These are open to the
public and professionals as part of the ever-expanding
need to tap into additional student populations.

The *National Committee for Prevention of Child Abuse*
has also recently merged local chapters of *Parents Anonymous* and *Committees for Prevention of Child Abuse* into

one group called *Friends for the Prevention of Child Abuse*. Currently, thriteen states have merged their state chapters of Parents Anonymous and the National Committee for Prevention of Child Abuse into the one group, having as its goals:

1. Stimulating greater public awareness of child abuse prevention.
2. Advocating for public and private sector child abuse prevention policies and procedures.
3. Developing, strengthening, and expanding child abuse prevention activities.
4. Strengthening relationships among organizations working to prevent child abuse.

Drawing upon the skills of trained professionals and volunteers, prevention programs from the *Friends for the Prevention of Child Abuse* help families and the community through support, linkage with valuable resources, and parent education. For more information about weekly meetings of the *Friends for the Prevention of Child Abuse*, consult your local newspaper, which often contains a special special section listing community groups. A sampling of typical programs available from the Friends group includes:

Parents Anonymous: Self-help support groups for parents who have either been abusive, or believe that they may become abusive because of the stresses in their lives.

Kids On The Block: A life-size puppet program that teaches young school children about child abuse.

New Parenting: Education material that is distributed to first-time parents providing information on community resources and child development. This program is often supported by volunteers who visit new parents at local hospitals to give the program a personal touch.

Professional/Parent Workshops and Conferences: Ongoing training for professionals and parents on parenting and child abuse prevention issues.

National Hotline: Child Abuse: 1-800-422-4453
A 24-hour toll free telephone number that will furnish information on child abuse and make referrals to appropriate prevention resources.

A parent might also consider these twelve suggestions for maintaining self-control and composure in situations involving child discipline. They were prepared by the *National Committee for Prevention of Child Abuse*.

1. Take a deep breath. And another. Then remember *you* are the adult.
2. Close your eyes and imagine you're hearing what your child is about to hear.
3. Press your lips together and count to ten. Or better yet, to twenty.
4. Put your child in a time-out chair. (Remember the rule: one time-out minute for each year of age.)
5. Put yourself in a time-out chair. Think about why you are angry: Is it your child, or is your child simply a convenient target for your anger?
6. Phone a friend.
7. If someone can watch the children, go outside and take a walk.
8. Take a hot bath or splash cold water on your face.
9. Hug a pillow.
10. Turn on some music. Maybe even sing along.
11. Pick up a pencil and write down as many helpful words as you can think of. Save the list.

12. Write a letter to the *National Committee for Prevention of Child Abuse* (Box 2866L, Chicago, IL 60690) asking for child abuse prevention information.

The telephone book yellow pages (and white-page business sections or residences) provide an easy access to helping. Telephoning pastors, rabbis, or others for appointments or referral information may be appropriate. Many larger companies/corporations provide Employee Assistance Programs for employees. A telephone call to that office or to the personnel office provides confidential information or assistance. The telephone book lists professional help in the yellow pages (or white) under counselor, psychologist, marriage and family therapy and individual professionals by name or their firm's name. Local mental health centers/associations are typically in the white-page business sections of the telephone book, as is a community referral service, if one exists.

Your local community referral service also may publish a low-cost directory of community services available in your area. The closest available domestic violence shelter/center may be located through Employee Assistance Programs, private practitioners, mental health centers/associations, close friends or relatives, ministers, or the community referral service. Self-help mutual support groups, if they exist in the community, are advertised regularly in your local newspapers.

Those working in the field also have a general knowledge of such self-help and problem-centered groups, their meeting days, places, and times, and telephone numbers. Currently, there are thirty-two self-help mutual support group clearinghouses operating in the United States, Canada, Europe, and Japan, with the predominant number (26) in the United States. The number of specific groups, such as *Alcoholics Anonymous* and *Toughlove*, a group for parents troubled by their teenagers' behavior, is several times that amount. There is an excellent self-help source-book available for a nominal fee ($10.00, first class postage, $9.00 book-rate postage) from St. Clares-Riverside Medical Center. Their address and telephone numbers are as follows: Self-Help Clearinghouse, ATTN: *Sourcebook*, St. Clares-Riverside Medical Center, Denville, NJ 07834. Telephones, inside NJ, (201) 625-9053 or 1-800-367-6274; outside NJ, (201) 625-9565.

WINDOWS
Discipline, Values and Reason

It is said that beauty is in the eye of the beholder. We could agree on a standard of beauty, but we would quickly disagree over who had the prettiest baby. So too are there vast differences in the ways parents raise their children. Knowing this, a message I have tried to present in *A Fine Line* is that effective parenting cannot be done by using a "cookbook." Parenting should not bog down in questions about how to best control a child's every act.

Instead, parents need a window on the world, a point of view they wish to maintain and pass on. As parents, what greater joy and feeling of satisfaction is there in life than to see your children grow into well-disciplined, productive and loving adults? The opposite is the absence of self-discipline and self-direction, where one's will must prevail, and where everyone must have what they want and have it now. This nation's courts and jails are filled with those who never learned self-discipline. If a parent has no goals and values (what's important in life, how others should be treated, attitudes toward work and responsibilities) to provide a child direction, then the child, not the parent, is in control.

Discipline is a parental requirement, but discipline should not be confused with harsh and negative punishment. The point of parental discipline is for the child to develop *self-discipline*. Getting there requires time and quality relationships between parents and children.

Often we, as parents, get caught up in "the now." Or our face-saving need for a triumphant resolve overcomes the value in the lesson to be taught. Many parents believe that children must be dealt with promptly; they must see that adults have all the answers and they must obey immediately. Then the values that drive behavior become today's events and time becomes the essence.

But there is another side, the child's. "What am I about to do and why?" That is a far different question than, "What did I do and what will happen to me now?" In this book I have asked parents to consider the values they are teaching. To "just say no to drugs" isn't an effective value upon which decisions are made. Recognizing that drugs are self-destructive and reduce one's control over life—and wishing to avoid this—is a value.

Value-based discipline asks the parent to view childhood as a living laboratory. In this laboratory children have the opportunity to develop decision-making skills and to try them out in confronting life's problems. Childhood is a chance for children to made decisions under the guided supervision of parents. But what if they don't want their parents' input? Growing up means gaining independent decision-making ability. They shouldn't want their parents' input unless they cannot handle a decision themselves. Rational decision-making is not learned by a given birthday. It is learned as children practice being children through the interactions of the parent-child relationship.

EASIER OR BEST?

"How do I get my child to obey?" is the question raised most frequently in parenting groups. Then comes the response, "It's easier for me to do it, than to tell him to do it." The "it" can be cleaning a room or doing the dishes, or completing homework, or observing a quiet time. Some parents can't seem to lower their speed, their pace, their need for efficiency, to take time to teach their children through a time-honored process: reasoning and communicating personal values. This leads to serious problems for the family now, and for the children later in life.

Children are born with minds. Nature guides the developmental process of thinking and learning. However, the contents of the mind, such as the values and beliefs that will guide their emotional responses, are all learned, especially through modeling parents and significant others. The power of modeling is much greater than was understood just a few years ago.

Children arrange the values they learn into belief systems. Developing a personal belief system involves screening out messages posing as values but that are merely controlling, or directing. Children question statements by parents that make no sense except to regulate. A parent who says, "do it because I say so," has not taught a value. This parent has given a directive and can anticipate that it will be challenged at some point. That parent is now in the position of enforcing that value.

A parent who explains why a behavior makes sense in terms of the child's responsibility to self and others teaches a value. While words *may* teach a child, a parent's behavior automatically provides a child with learning. Children will quickly understand and practice honesty, integrity, loyalty, and responsibility toward others when they see parents use these values every day. These children will be strengthened.

In working with incarcerated adults, it is amazing how frequently they say that their parents, especially their fathers, challenged rules, broke rules, and failed to develop rules. In examining the lives of over one hundred male spouse abusers, for example, I noted three common themes. These men (1) lacked a positive male role model; (2) felt controlled by others; and (3) were poor decision makers. They were often threatened by their families, feeling inferior to their wives whom they wished to control, and they became frustrated in some major avenue of life's pursuit. Their limited, poor decision-making capability often resulted in an inability to resolve conflict.

That conflict could come from work, or it could result from competition for the affection of their spouse. It could be they felt deprived of the attention that was vital to them, in their own immature response to life. Domestic violence is often committed in the absence of control and in the presence of anger, even rage. *These emotions are, however, only the trigger. What they trigger is a response system devoid of values.*

Where does discipline begin? Children are not chattel, nor are they little adults who are to conform to the ever-changing whims of their parents. Children must learn rules. They must learn to be consistently obedient to the values contained in those rules, and to demonstrate that lesson by practicing respect for others. Discipline begins with parents modeling self-discipline and the expression of positive regard for one another. But it is not for the parents' sake. It is for the children, preparing them for adult living and the responsibility of relationships with others, the basis of a civilized community.

Discipline is learned by hearing and seeing the behaviors of others who are in meaningful relationships and internalizing these as self-control. Discipline has a natural progression. It begins in the mouths of the parents; is received as meaningful in the ear of the child; and then becomes incorporated as a value that provides self-control for the person. It is reinforced by seeing it practiced in the family.

No Discipline Without Values

One thing we can count on is that not all human actions are constructive or responsible. People are not god-like, perfect creatures. All of us are self-serving. The person we tend to like the best is ourselves and the person we think about the most is ourselves. Often the people we like the least are those for or to whom we feel responsible. Children are born as willful beings, and they grow in the need for self-recognition. The great American society has supported to an abnormal degree this need in all of us to be self-serving, to state our needs and fulfill them. The mark of the "me generation" is that it seeks immediate self-gratification.

The definition of discipline is to teach, through reason, a respect for others—for the common good. Discipline recognizes others' needs, even if they overshadow ours. Discipline without values is punishment, merely a means of controlling others. Punishment in anger teaches anger. Uncontrolled punishment, as a response of rage, teaches violence and sets abuse of others into motion for another generation. It is said that even Satan quotes scripture, and it is clearly true that many people justify neglecting and controlling children by any means available. But New Testament teachings address parental responsibility and parental expression as an act of love (nurturing), caring, and responsibility.

Discipline must be taught as control of self. Therefore it must be taught as reason, through the process of reasoning. Rules for rules' sake are external control measures. Rules should be taught from birth, as values that are principles to guide our behaviors. Think of the difference in saying to a ten-year-old, "Do it because I say so," in contrast to asking the question, "What is the rule? Why do we have that rule?" The child who is told what to do, without reason, will eventually test the rules.

Teaching reason is not saying to a child, "Now, do it this way," or "Do it my way." Reasoning is a thought-provoking interaction requiring time for a child to see the entire scheme. It is an example of Gestalt learning, which means that the sum of the pieces must be incorporated into the whole of what is to be learned.

For many parents, time and patience are lost commodities, lost in a world that runs at a hectic pace and values the product and not the process. "Isn't he a nice little boy. So well mannered!" That is a result of work, of teaching values and decision making. It does not require much time to say to a child, "Now hear this; this is an order; you will comply." It does take time to request that children listen and learn by interacting, sharing views, and offering opinions, explaining what they would do and trying to foresee the consequences. It takes time to reason through something to see why it is so. It does not take time to order someone or to do it for them.

Some parents confuse the teaching of reasoning with negotiation. Parents may say "It's okay, if you don't get caught" or "It's okay, but just this once." At other times parents may try to adopt practices that seem to work for others—themes from movies and TV shows, printed media, and local conventional wisdom. None of these reflect value learning, nor do they teach reasoning and independent decision-making skills. They teach manipulation, and how to get by with the least possible compliance.

Children model their behavior after adults. Parents who are inconsistent, a natural result of trying to control behavior with their emotions, set an emotional tone within their children. Children in this controlling, or rejecting, or uncertain world respond by manipulating and testing limits. Their search is for the elusive bedrock of the parents' beliefs and feelings for them.

Parents who do not have well-developed behavioral goals for their children often are inconsistent. They speak time and place messages (responses to immediate situations) to their children instead of stressing broader and lasting values. Parents who do not possess strong positive values are likely to let their children go too far in self-direction. Trying to discover any limits required by these parents—to find and understand the rules—a child may pass the limits of parental tolerance. Parents who are inconsistent or lack a strong, well-developed and clearly communicated value system find their children becoming assertive or challenging when it is least acceptable. Then these parents show their anger, acting from strong emotion. They cross the line into child abuse.

CHANGING ATTITUDES

Have recent generations of Americans, through constant wars, security consciousness, and industrial misuse of the environment, altered their attitudes toward long-term human and environmental relationships? Has the importance of values and respect for relationships been redefined by a personal and national philosophy that says the only responsibility I have is to me?

Attitudes toward society in America today are changing. It seems that the "me" generation has found that "easier is better" and has redefined the ultimate human experience in these terms. Thus, we accept that children spend a minimum of three hours each day in front of the television, and two hours each month with their fathers; and that disposable diapers are better than cloth, though they have become a major source of dioxin.

Perhaps to the "me" generation it is impossible to be both a product of it and a contributor. Perhaps bright, capable people don't have the interest in child rearing they once had. Perhaps we are no longer concerned with what value system the next generation develops, because technology is perceived as the solution to all problems.

Quality time for children or family has been seriously disregarded. After all, building and maintaining relationships is hard work. It is easier to do for a child than to teach the child. It is easier to control than to teach reason. It is easier to find the answer in a pill or powder than to grope through the daily tedium of life trying to find harmony, productiveness, and moderation. These values translate into behaviors necessary for human support relationships.

Could it be that in our frantic search for security we have overlooked stability? Is there a metaphorical relationship between "no deposit, no return" and short, cheap relationships that are easy and not very meaningful? Is there a relationship between the thousands of cheap junky petrochemical items and good quality leather, a renewable and biodegradable resource that will last for years? Today we seem to choose based on form and not on function. If we don't like a relationship, then we will get a new one.

Today I see much more pulling apart than I see pulling together. Relationship maintenance may be hard work but it yields maximum benefits.

The issue is that for every measure of comfort there is a byproduct. Our society has learned to live easily with bad products and bad waste. This suggests that destructiveness in human relationships (therefore in human society and ultimately in the ecosystem) is acceptable. In the past, the balances in nature and human relationships have been slow to change, thus permitting adaptation. Today, however, the speed of individual, societal, and environmental changes makes the term "stability" suspect, and obsolete.

Although there is no security in this life, there can be stability through human understanding. We attain this by strengthening our relationship with a creator, creating bonds with positive human relationships, and respecting nature. Thus, through relationships we discover a common good.

DISTORTIONS OF LOVE

The sexual abuse of children is an emotion-charged subject, a universally condemned form of abuse. Incest or sexual practices of any kind with minors violate the laws and morals of our society. Values again are implicated.

Sex is a biological act expressing the emotions of physical attraction. The internal control for sexual expression is in a strong positive value sense associated with the responsibility of love and marriage. Sexual behavior entails responsibilities: selfless responsibilities for the feelings of another, responsibilities for any product resulting from that act, responsibilities for kindness and consideration within the act. These responsibilities are value-based and altruistic, not the selfish values that appear to threaten modern American society. The "me generation," the theme of modern adult life——doing what feels good, seeking adventure and hedonistic self-expression, while emulating the lives of television and movie characters——provides a sharp contrast to the values required for a healthful sexuality.

Just what are the values of an adult who sexually abuses a child? Further still, what are the values of that same adult who orders a child to be silent about such abuses, that telling anyone, will only bring additional hurt and shame? What are the values present when an adult is driven to take advantage of a child he or she has responsibility for teaching? But then that may be the point. Far too many adults view children as miniature adults. Such people disregard their responsibility for teaching children, for modeling the display of caring, loving, and emotional support. Other adults simply feel the power to control, as if they own the children and therefore have a license to do to them as they please.

Even the strongest attraction, expressed as the feeling we call love, requires discipline. If I tell a young woman, "I love you," it should mean that I respect you and your wishes, that I want to be in a serious relationship with you, one where I place your needs above all others. Our mutual needs will be expressed as a strong desire to work and live together through a communication bond that allows us the freedom to express personal fears, aspirations, beliefs, and desires. It is in that context that a relationship grows and develops, serving the people who contribute to it. As they grow so does the relationship.

Let's contrast that with a man attracted to a woman by one thing, her physical attributes. The man expresses his biological desire in the same statement, "I love you." What may follow is an effort to dominate that person for personal satisfaction. It might go something like this, "I love you, therefore it is legitimate that I can have you sexually. And, if you reject my sexual overtures then you are rejecting my love." That places a woman in a difficult situation. She is flattered by the attention and overwhelmed with the infatuation. She acknowledges his love and may well return feelings of trust and submission. The only mutual need is sexual gratification. Indeed, there may be nothing else that these two human beings have in common. Any other goals or desires to work together will soon become a master/servant relationship: I, the master; you, the submissive slave if you love me. I will give the orders and you will comply. Love is now a word that means control.

What is exercised here is not selfless giving, but control based on "because I want it." Marriages emerging from these conditions soon fail (maybe they never began). Dissatisfaction overshadows the physical attraction and replaces it with animosity. As I have described in this book, the root cause of uncontrolled anger, a force behind child abuse, is when an experience does not meet the promise held for it.

Many women idealize marriage and prepare for it as young girls, playing house and caring for their dolls. To find a few years later that the only interest a husband has in them is for the service they render is a severe shattering of that ideal. The result is anger, anger that may be expressed toward the product of that union: the children.

Diostortions in love also appear as dependent attachments to children, attachments that enable parents to move beyond their own feelings of inadequate love, expressed as overprotection of their children. These dependent (codependent) parents fail to provide positive disciplinary guidance for their children. The controlling and growth-stifling behaviors that often accompany these faulty psychological attachments can be as damaging as physical abuse. But they are harder to identify and much more difficult to treat.

Rejection and neglect, the absence of expressions of parental love, is the child abuse that often goes unnoticed. Yet parental rejection is child abuse. When we don't see evidence of physical abuse, or feel the outrage that incestuous behaviors bring, we often overlook the emotional (and physical) neglect that leaves scars. Neglect denies children the emotional interactions they need for growth. Neglect distorts the very framework of a child's emotional response mechanism. It duplicates, in keeping with its physical abuse counterparts, a cycle that all too often will reappear in the next generation.

RELIEVING THE PRESSURE

Many enter into the act of rearing children with little forethought or preparation. Some have little money, but a mountain of other personal, social, vocational, and marital problems. Into their lives it seldom rains, unless it pours. Parents fitting this description need help. They need the support of structured groups to hear and reassure them. This is support that stands in contrast to their own parents, or to a spouse, who may not care to understand how to manage children's behavior other than by traditional practices.

Human service agencies have learned the importance of teaching parenting skills, especially when conflict and stress exist within the home. The above paragraph should not read as if the only parents who need help are those with financial or multiple life problems. I am reminded of an experienced social worker who spent her life in a Department of Human Services working with child care. She was skillful in teaching others to manage difficult child placement problems, many of which were brought on by child abuse. This capable professional married, in her mid-thirties, a very busy physician. When her son was born, he appeared immediately to be different. He was not a quiet, obedient child. From birth he had colic, was restless and slept little.

This hyperactivity increased with age. As he began to walk, he began to destroy everything in his path; when he began to talk, he never stopped. This child had an attention deficit disorder, which placed unusual and great stress on his mother. Her parents adored the boy and told her to leave him alone, the problem was her, not him. Her husband's parents thought there must be some defect in *her* family.

The father was seldom home, and when he came home he wanted just to eat and relax. He did not want to hear about a boy who was threatening to destroy his marriage. The mother was alone with a deep well of feelings, many of them negative and contrary to the strong feelings of attachment she wanted to show. As a result, she vacillated between overcontrol (harsh punishment) and overindulgence of the child's whims.

At a preschool clinic, a teacher observed that the child was hyperactive. The mother took the boy to a pediatrician, who referred him to a psychologist. After consulting with the psychologist she joined a support group of preschool mothers with Attention Disorder Deficit children. With support from this group, she developed new resolve that she could manage the problem. And with that resolve, and the support of others who understood, came the ability to hear needed child management and coping strategies. She no longer believed she was "losing her mind."

In another case, it was a pleasure to hear a young rural Appalachian mother and her mother interact with one another and with me as I obtained a developmental history. The reason for the referral was a suspected developmental disability that placed the child at academic risk. The young woman could see only the child's immediate needs. And, she was overwhelmed by them. Her mother, having raised a large family, could foresee the child's development through the growth years and into adulthood. She was there for her daughter. She provided a support that quieted the daughter's overwrought emotions and opened the door to understanding.

Can you imagine so much emotional pain that you cannot connect with anyone? When you are alone in pain, your loneliness is a black despair. The depression is real, it is severe, and it requires concentrated and comprehensive professional management. It is probably easier to understand stresses that are overwhelming. These seem to settle on us like a heavy suit of clothes and produce emotional states that reduces our reason, causing the smallest aspect of life to be menacing and confusing. A person alone and in pain needs the increased personal awareness that counseling supports provide, followed by group support offering information and understanding.

Sometimes emotional pain or emotional discomfort can be strong enough to reduce or even eliminate the ability to receive and use information. Sometimes, in the presence of intense emotions, or even the frustration resulting from an implied fear of failing (our families, ourselves, and especially our children), we can not possibly react wisely to additional information. In that moment we need the comfort and unconditional positive regard that a professional or trained peer counselor who has "been there" knows how to offer.

Support can simply be good information in a judgement-free environment. Parenting skills can be freely examined when supportive relationships are established and the parent is heard. Often, before we can hear others, *we* need to be heard. Most of us have already been judged harshly by others and by ourselves. Support groups soften and make human our self-criticism while encouraging new resolve and more effective parenting.

Human support should be viewed as a parenting safety net providing the courage and confidence to try again. It should be seen as a door that can be opened, letting in new and vital information. And it should provide a non-rejecting, nonjudgmental relationship that promotes a sense of well-being, even in a sea of turmoil; a support system that says, "Keep trying."

TWO CHOICES

What do we want for our children? In discipline there are two choices. One is to compel our children to fit into the family, and ultimately society, by telling them what is expected and seeing to it that they conform. Parents set the rules and children comply or suffer painful consequences. This choice does not require parents to maintain a special relationship with the child. It does not require parents to be models. It does not require parents to give up anything they want. It only requires respect for rules, because they are absolute, and the adult power that enforces them absolutely.

The other choice asks more of parents. Every day is seen as a chance to develop a deeper relationship with the child, to show the child new things and to provide new opportunities for learning. Parents teach reasoning not rules, reasoning based on values that require a respect for others. To respect others one must learn self-discipline. It is not good enough to merely serve oneself and do what feels good now.

With this choice, childhood is seen also as a chance to learn that life has a purpose. That purpose is for us to enrich the attachment among all living things, in relationships beyond ourselves. Life is seen as a responsibility requiring care of the environment and an abiding love of all life. If punishment requires control of others, then this love offers each generation new hope to be more than we now are.

In choosing our way of parenting we enact our meaning of love.

NOTES on Sources

DIFFERENCES: *Punishment or Discipline?*

1. National Center for Health Statistics, *Vital Statistics of the United States* (Washington, DC: Government Printing Office, 1984), 36-37.
2. Dennis P. Hogan, *Transitions and Social Change: The Early Lives of American Men* (New York: Academic Press, 1981), 291. Mariani amplified the result of skipping the natural progression of these stages into implications for the poor development of parenting skills. See Margaret Marini, "The Order of Events in the Transition of Adulthood," *Sociology of Education* 57 (April 1984): 63-84.
3. Kazuo Yamaguchi and Denise Kandel, "Drug Use and Other Determinants of Premarital Pregnancy and Its Outcome: A Dynamic Analysis of Competing Life Events." *Journal of Marriage and the Family* 49 (May 1987): 257-270.
4. John E. Donovan and Richard Jessor, "Structure of Behavior in Adolescence and Young Adulthood." *Journal of Consulting and Clinical Psychology* 53 (December 1985): 890-904.
5. William I. Thompson, *At the Edge of History* (New York: Harper & Row, 1971), 180.

TRADITIONS: *Origins of a Dangerous Tool*

1. Bruno Bettleheim, *A Home for the Heart,* 1st ed. (New York: Knopf, 1974), 317.
2. Laurence Kolberg, David Ricks, and John Snarey, "Childhood Development as a Predictor of Adulthood," *Genetic Psychology Monograph* 110 (January 1984): 91-172.

3. Emile Durkheim, *The Rules of Sociological Method* (Chicago: The University of Chicago Press, 1938), 112.

4. Alfred Ewing, *The Morality of Punishment: Philosophical Perspectives on Punishment* (London: K. Paul, Trench, Truber & Co. Ltd, 1929), 223.

5. Quoted passages are from, respectively, Gen. 4:14(AV), Prov. 3:12(AV), and Heb. 12:7-8(AV) Greek and Roman law also dictated retribution, although Plato's Republic clearly reflects the philosopher's dissatisfaction with retribution-based punishment as he sought a more perfect world. It is amazing that post-Renaissance Europe and England were still drawing on the ancient Biblical dictum of "an eye for an eye and a tooth for a tooth." Neither St. Thomas Aquinas nor Immanuel Kant found fault with societal practice of retribution for retribution's sake. In his *Philosophy of Law*, Kant wrote that punishment can never be administered merely to promote another good, but must always be imposed simply because the individual punished has committed a crime. He saw the moral value of social retribution inseparable from the retribution itself. See Immanuel Kant, *The Philosophy of Law: Philosophical Perspectives on Punishment*, trans. W. Hastie (Edinburgh & London: T.T. Clark, 1887), 162.

6. John D. Mabbott, *The State and the Citizen: An Introduction to Political Philosophy,* 2nd ed. (London: Hutchinson, 1967), 175.

7. Punishment ". . . must in all cases be imposed only because the individual on whom it is inflicted has committed a crime" (Kant, *The Philosophy of Law,* 217). Mabbott noted that the failure to respect the rights of others extinguishes an individual's own rights, thus making him a proper subject of punishment. The state (or parent) has the moral responsibility to injure him as he has injured others (Mabbott, *The State and the Citizen*, 175).

8. Nigel Walker examined the penal aspects of our laws and courts, noting that retribution is the basis of our legal system (Nigel Walker, Varieties of Retributivism: *Contemporary Punishment* [Notre Dame: University of Notre Dame Press,

1966], 83-92). He went on to say, "But to abandon it completely is politically out of the question" (*Ibid.*, 86).

9. Stanley Benn and Richard Peters, *Social Principles and the Democratic State: Philosophical Perspectives on Punishment* (London: George Allen and Unwin Ltd., 1959), 182-183.

ABUSE AND NEGLECT: *A Tragedy of Generations*

1. John Caffey, "Multiple Fractures in the Long Bones of Infants Suffering from Chronic Subdural Hematoma," *American Journal of Roentgenology, Radium Therapy, and Nuclear Medicine* 56 (September 1946): 163-173.

2. C. Henry Kempe, et al., "The Battered Child Syndrome," *Journal of the American Medical Association* 181 (February 1962): 17-24.

3. David R. Gil, *Child Abuse and Violence* (New York: AMS Press, 1979), 614. See also: David R. Gil, *Violence Against Children: Physical Child Abuse in the United States* (Cambridge, MA: Harvard University Press, 1970), 204, and Richard J. Gelles and Claire P. Cornell, *Intimate Violence in Families* (Newbury Park: Sage, 1990), 159.

4. American Humane Association, *Reports of Child Abuse and Neglect Continue to Increase in 1985* (Denver, CO: Author, 1986), 4-6.

5. John Whiting et al., "Infanticide," *Society for Cross-Cultural Research Newsletter* 5 (December 1977): 1-6.

6. R. C. Herrenkohl and E. C. Herrenkohl, "Some Antecedents and Developmental Consequences of Child Maltreatment," *New Directions for Child Development* 11 (March 1981): 57-76.

7. *Ibid*, 59.

8. Nev. Rev. Stat. §200.5011(2), (1983).

9. It is not uncommon to find parents who punish harshly if a child steals, but who themselves steal from the stores in which they shop regularly. In some cases, children learn that the values to live by are "It is all right to do it; just don't get caught."

10. Arizona, New Hampshire, and Wisconsin describe children's reactions using language such as: severe anxiety, depression, withdrawal, or untoward aggressive behaviors as evidenced in serious emotional damage. New Hampshire has rather explicit language, identifying psychological injury by the display of symptoms of emotional problems generally recognized to result from consistent mistreatment or neglect.

New York gives its child service providers considerable decision-making authority. The statute defines a neglected child as one whose mental or emotional condition or well-being has been impaired or is in imminent danger of becoming impaired due to the failure of the parent or guardian to exercise a minimum of reasonable care. Maryland describes a neglected child as one who has suffered significant mental harm or injury from parents or guardians or their failure to provide proper care and attention.

Nebraska, New Jersey, Indiana, and Washington define abuse and neglect as any condition or situation that endangers the child's mental health. The New Jersey law reads "any mental or emotional condition (that) has been impaired or is in imminent danger of becoming impaired as the result of failure of his parents or guardians." Connecticut uses the term "emotional maltreatment." Iowa defines it as a child in need of treatment or assistance to cure or alleviate serious mental illness or disorders or emotional damage and whose parents are unable to provide such treatment. North Carolina statutes read "creates or allows to be created serious emotional damage to the juvenile and refuses to permit, provide or participate in treatment."

There are states such as North Dakota, that use the term "traumatic abuse"; Oregon's excellent definition reads "any mental injury to a child which includes observable and substantial impairments of the child's mental or psychological ability to function caused by cruelty to the child."

Alaska and Colorado are the only states who do not include the terms mental, psychological, and emotional or have other comparable terms in the language of their statutes.

11. Susan Creighton, *Trends in Child Abuse* (London: NSPCC, 1984), 266.

SEXUAL ABUSE: *A Toxic Relationship*

1. One study found that of 1,056 respondents questioned regarding childhood sexual abuse, 7.4% reported experiencing it (Glen A. Kercher and Marilyn McShane, *"The Prevalence of Child Sexual Abuse Victimization in an Adult Sample of Texas Residents,"* Child Abuse and Neglect 8: 495-501. Brenda J. Vander Mey reported that over 11% of the women in this country today, as represented in the population she sampled, had been sexually victimized during childhood (Brenda J. Vander Mey, "Adult-Child Incest: A Sample of Substantiated Cases," *Family Relations* 33 [October, 1984]: 549-557). A classic study is that of David Finkelhor (*Child Sexual Abuse: New Theory and Research* [New York: Free Press/Macmillan, 1984], 260.

2. Brenda Vander Mey, "Adult-Child Incest."

3. T. Baker studied college women (*Report on Reader Survey: Child Sex Abuse - "19" Confidential Survey,* [London: St. Georges Hospital, 1983, Mimeographed]). Another important study was conducted by Diana E. Russell ("The Prevalence and Seriousness of Incestuous Abuse: Step Fathers vs. Biological Fathers," *Child Abuse and Neglect* 8 [September 1984]: 15-22).

4. John Briere and Marsha Runtz, "Multivariate Correlates of Childhood Psychological and Physical Maltreatment Among University Women," *Child Abuse and Neglect* 12 (March 1988): 331-341.

5. Arthur C. Jaffe, Lucille Dynneson, and Robert Ten Bensel, "Sexual Abuse: An Epidemiological Study," *American Journal of Diseases of Children* 129 (June 1975): 689-692.

6. *Ibid.*, 689-692.

7. The accepted mean age is 7 to 8 years, and the modal age is in the 8 to 12 year range (Jaffe, Dynneson, and Ten Bensel, "Sexual Abuse: An Epidemiological Study," 689-690).

8. Laurence R. Ricci, "Medical Forensic Photography of the Sexually Abused Child," *Child Abuse and Neglect* 12 (March 1988): 305-310.

9. Christopher Ringwalt and JoAnne Earp, "Attributing Responsibility in Cases of Father-Daughter Sexual Abuse," *Child Abuse and Neglect* 12 (April 1988): 273-281.

10. Many studies place it in the ten- to twelve-year range, but it is clearly related to pubescent changes. Jaffe's study reports that the incidents increased rapidly over the mean age for females and decreased for males. Twenty-nine percent of the girls were over the age of twelve, and only sixteen percent of the boys were over the age of twelve. This age-sex relationship does seem to be a consistent finding (Jaffe, Dynneson, and Ten Bensel, "Sexual Abuse: An Epidemiological Study"), 689-692.

11. Norman Polansky et al., *Damaged Parents: An Anatomy of Child Neglect* (Chicago: The University of Chicago Press, 1981), 89.

12. Ringwalt and Earp, "Attributing Responsibility," 273-281.

13. *Ibid.*

14. *Ibid.*

15. Ricci, "Medical Forensic Photography," 305-310.

16. V. C. Schoettle, "Treatment of the Child Pornography Patient," *Journal of Psychiatry* 137 (November 1980): 1109-1110; Robert Burgess and James Garbarino, "Doing What Comes Naturally? An Evolutionary Perspective on Child Abuse," in *The Dark Side of Families*, ed. David Finkelhor et al. (Beverly Hills, CA: Sage, 1983), 88.

17. "The sexual misuse of male children is a poorly understood area of child abuse, replete with much misinformation and many myths . . . the dynamics of the sexual abuse of males have little in common with those involving females" (Joseph K. Fischoff, Charles Whilten, and Marvin G. Petit, "A Psychiatric Study of Mothers of Infants with Growth Failure Secondary to Maternal Deprivation," *Journal of Pediatrics* 79 [August 1971]: 209-215.

18. Davied Finkelhor, *Child Sexual Abuse: New Theory and Research* (New York: Free Press/Macmillan, 1984), 260.

19. A. Nicholas Groth reported that 85% of male perpetrators had themselves been victimized (*Men Who Rape: The Psychology of the Offender* [New York: Plenum, 1979], 227.

20. Ruth S. Kempe and C. Henry Kempe, *The Common Secret: Sexual Abuse of Children and Adolescents* (New York: W. H. Freeman, 1984), 284.

21. Charles Swift wrote, "A conspiracy of silence surrounds a boy who is sexually victimized. His victimization is proof that he has failed in one of the primary mandates of the masculine role - to defend himself. To share his trauma is to advertise his defeat and invite not only immediate humiliation, but continuing stigmatization" ("Sexual Victimization of Children: An Urban Mental Health Center Survey," *Victimology* 2 [February 1977]: 324).

22. See Stephen Grubman-Black, *Broken Boys/Mending Men: Recovery from Childhood Sexual Abuse* (Blue Ridge Summit, PA: HSI/TAB-McGraw-Hill, 1990).

23. See Vera Gallagher, *Becoming Whole Again: Help for Women Survivors of Childhood Sexual Abuse* (Blue Ridge Summit, PA: HSI/TAB-McGraw-Hill, 1990).

24. Finkelhor, *Child Sexual Abuse,* 260.

WHY? *The Origins of Child Abuse*

1. Richard Gelles was the first to offer a social psychological model to explain child abuse. Inherent in that explanation were the immediate precipitating situations, which can be drawn from among the vast array of possible antecedent causes of abuse (Gelles and Cornell, *Intimate Violence in Families*). David R. Gil refers to these as triggering contexts (Gil, *Child Abuse and Violence*). Murray Strauss, Richard Gelles, and Suzanne Steinmetz all refer to younger children's inability to reason and older children's refusal to reason as creating situations that are potentially vulnerable to violent parental reactions (Murray Strauss, Richard J. Gelles, and Suzanne Steinmetz, *Behind Closed Doors: Violence in the American Family* [Garden City, New York: Anchor Books, Doubleday, 1980], 301).

2. C. Henry Kempe summarized years of observations on infants and toddlers when he wrote that "When a child is abused, it is always at a point of crisis, often an apparently trivial one . . . the most frequent irritants are messy feeding, soiling (particularly when the parent's clothes get soiled) and intractable crying" Ruth S. Kempe and C. Henry Kempe, *Child Abuse,* [Cambridge MA: Harvard University Press, 1978], 136).

3. *Ibid.,* 136.

4. In support of this general observation in a more recent study, Alfred Kadushin and Judith Martin further examined the types of behaviors that are immediate precursors to physical abuse (*Child Abuse: An Interactional Event* [New York: Columbia University Press, 1981], 304.

5. Joanne Giovannoni and Rosiha M. Becerra, *Defining Child Abuse* (New York: Free Press, 1979), 302.

6. National Center on Child Abuse and Neglect, *National Study of the Incidence and Severity of Child Abuse and Neglect.* Department of Health and Human Services Publication No. (OHDS) 81-30325 (Washington, DC: Author, 1981), 1-26.

7. *Ibid,* 1-26.

8. Elizabeth Elmer, "A Follow-Up Study of Traumatized Children," *Pediatrics* 59 (December 1977): 273-279.

9. Gil, *Child Abuse and Violence*. In a similar study, a British researcher reported that twenty-nine percent of mothers of young physically abused children were unmarried. In thirty-five percent of abuse cases the biological father was absent from the home.

10. Elizabeth Elmer, "Traumatized Children, Chronic Illness, and Poverty," in *The Social Context of Child Abuse and Neglect,* ed. Leon Pelton (New York: Human Sciences Press, 1981), 185-227.

11. Gil, *Child Abuse and Violence*.

12. David Gutman, "Oedipus and the Aging Male: A Comparative Perspective," *The Psychoanalytic Review* 73 (Winter 1986): 541-552.

13. I. Laurie, "Family Dynamics and the Abuse of Adolescents," *Child Abuse and Neglect* 3 (May 1979): 967-974.

14. Richard Lerner, "Children as Producers of their own Environments," *Developmental Review* 2 (Spring 1982): 342-370.

15. David M. Bousha and Craig T. Twentyman, "Mother-Child Interactional Style in Abuse, Neglect, and Control Groups: Naturalistic Observations in the Home," *Journal of Abnormal Psychology* 93 (February 1984): 106-114.

16. Jeanne M. Giovannoni and Alfred Billingsley, "Child Neglect Among the Poor: A Study of Parental Adequacy in Families of Three Ethnic Groups," *Child Welfare* 49 (March 1970): 196-204.

17. N. Z. Polansky, C. Hally, and N. A. Polansky, *Profile of Neglect: A Survey of the State of Knowledge of Child Neglect* (Washington, DC: U.S. Department of Health, Education and Welfare, 1976), 26.

18. J. Robert Havighurst is a major explainer of the stages of development (*Schools Face New Desegregation Phase,* [Nation's Schools, 1966]). Other prominent researchers described various aspects of development. Erikson used the term "psycho-social crisis" to refer to the child's psychological efforts to adjust to the demands of the social environment at each stage of development. "Crisis" in this context describes normal stresses and strains, not extraordinary ones (Eric H. Erikson, *Identity, Youth, and Crisis,* [New York: Norton, 1968], 366.

19. William James, *The Principles of Psychology* (New York: Henry Holt and Co., 1890), 391.

ATTACHMENT OR NEGLECT? *The Parent-Child Relationship*

1. Barton D. Schmitt conducted research on parents' language that leads to emotional abuse ("Seven Deadly Sins of Childhood: Advising Parents About Difficult Developmental Phases," *Child Abuse and Neglect* 11 [December 1987]: 421-432.); also see Christina Christopolous, John D. Bonvillian, and Patricia M. Crittenden, "Maternal Language Input and Child Maltreatment," *Infant Mental Health Journal* 9 (Winter 1988): 4.

2. Interestingly enough, the amount of learned behavior that is associated with parenting practices has resulted in Erikson drawing a sharp comparison between post-traumatic stress disorders observed in POWs and the continuing inability of those same children now, as adults, to display nurturing attachment in their parent-child relationships. See Erickson, *Identity, Youth, and Crisis*.

3. Ray E. Helfer, "The Perinatal Period, A Window of Opportunity for Enhancing Parent-Infant Communications: An Approach to Prevention," *Child Abuse and Neglect* 11: 565-579.

4. Barbara Merrill, *An Ounce of Prevention: Child Protection*. Training in Abuse Prevention (Charleston, WV: West Virginia Committee for Prevention of Child Abuse, Inc., 1986), 565-579.

5. Since 1977, child abuse has expanded from a restricted definition of physical abuse to include a wider array of caretaker behaviors. Often an occurrence in reality will not elicit a public reaction until a useful term is found that conveys the problem at a level upon which it cannot be tolerated by the conscience of the society at large (Stephen J. Pfohl, "The Discovery of Child Abuse," *Social Problems* 24 [February 1977]: 310-323). Tierney reported that the term wife-battering induced our social order to judge it and opt to support battered women (Kathleen Tierney and David Corwin, "Exploring Intra-Familial Child Sexual Abuse: A Systems Approach," in *The Dark Side of Families*, ed. David Finkelhor et al.) Deviant sexual practices within the bonds of marriage were not considered earth-shaking until Russell developed the concept of marital rape (*Sexual Exploitation: Rape, Child Sexual Abuse, and Workplace Harassment* [Beverly Hills, CA: Sage Library of Social Research*, 1984], 155). Jeanne Giovannoni and Rosina M. Becerra have also studied the social perception of various types of abuse *(Defining Child Abuse,* [New York: Free Press, 1979], 302.

6. John Bowlby, *Attachment and Loss* (New York: Basic Books, 1969), vol 1, "Attachment" (New York: Basic Books, 1969), 389; Brandt F. Steele, "Psychodynamic Factors in Child Abuse," in *The Battered Child,* 3rd ed., ed. C. Henry Kempe

and Ray Helfer (Chicago: University of Chicago Press, 1980), 188. Joan Kaufman and Edward Zigler recently declared that ". . . parents or other caretakers who maltreat babies were themselves neglected in their earliest years." They estimate the true rate of intergenerational transmission of neglect to be about thirty percent. This is five times the rate of maltreatment in the population at large (*Do Abused Children Become Abusive Parents?* [Unpublished manuscript, 1986], 26).

7. Richard Bach, *Jonathan Livingston Seagull* (New York: MacMillan, 1970).

8. John J. Spinetta and David Rigler, "The Child Abusing Parent: A Psychological Review," *Psychological Bulletin* 77 (April 1972): 296-304. In 1989, Elaine Walker, Geraldine Downey, and Andrea Bergman found a strong relationship between psychopathology in parents, maltreatment in families, and behavioral problems in children. Their model suggests that parents suffering from psychiatric control factors show a much higher than normal rate of maltreatment of their children. The significant impact occurs over time, with these children displaying greater frequency and duration of behavioral problems ("The Effects of Parental Psychopathology and Maltreatment on Child Behavior: A Test of the Diathesis-Stress Model," *Child Development* 60 [February 1989]: 15-24).

9. Ann M. Frodi, "Child Abusers' Responses to Infant Smiles and Cries," *Child Development* 52 (March 1980): 238-241.

10. These recent research findings support Bowlby's attachment framework. Bowlby hypothesized that parents have an internal working framework of child rearing. One of the highlights of John Bowlby's work is that children begin to construct relationship models as early as the first year of life (Bowlby, *Attachment and Loss*).

11. In an early study, Spinetta and Rigler ("The Child Abusing Parent") found that the majority of nonnurturing mothers were unable to perceive the needs of their children accurately, were emotionally disturbed, showed problematic object relations, and had a limited capacity for concern. Extended

families, blended families, and marital problems are a major source of conflict, tension, and loneliness. Howard Dubowitz reported that dependency, poor self-esteem, and limited empathy are the most common factors identified with mothers of children who fail to thrive (*Child Maltreatment in the United States: Etiology, Impact, and Prevention,* Background paper prepared for the Congress of the United States [Washington: Office of Technology Assessment, 1986], 128.

12. One recent study reported that 82 percent of the emotionally maltreated infants at 12 months of age demonstrated disorganized and disoriented attachments (Vicki Carlson et al., "Disorganized/disoriented attachment relationships in maltreated infants," *Developmental Psychology* 25 [May, 1989]: 525-531). Mary Main and Petra Hess suggest that fear interjected into the caregiver-child relationship is fundamental to developing a disorganized/disoriented attachment (*Lack of Resolution of Mourning in Adulthood and its Relationship to Infant Disorganization: Some Speculations Regarding Casual Mechanisms, Attachment During the Preschool Years,* [Chicago: University of Chicago Press, in press].

13. Frodi, "Child Abuser's Responses."

14. M. R. Brassard, R. Germain, and S. N. Hart reported that emotionally abused and neglected children scored lower on self-esteem and prosocial behaviors and higher on aggressiveness and withdrawn behaviors. These losses in self-esteem and impaired capacity to negotiate peer relationships at each developmental stage limit later social and academic interactions (*Psychological Maltreatment of Children and Young,* [New York: Pergammon Press, 1987], 232. Alan L. Sroufe et al. report that maltreated children prefer to confine their interaction to other maltreated children in freeplay ("Generational Boundary Dissolution between Mothers and their Preschool Children," *Child Development* 56 [April 1985]: 317-325). In the only controlled study of school-age maltreated children, maltreated children were found to interact less and display less affect than their peers (R. Jacobson and G. Straker, "Peer Group Interaction of Physically Abused

Children," *Child Abuse and Neglect* 6 [June 1982]: 321-327).

15. Kempe, *Child Abuse*, 21.
16. National Center on Child Abuse and Neglect, *National Study*.
17. Cantwell offers another link. Negative family patterns tend to generate adolescent conduct problems, which further threaten child-parent relationships and cause the adolescent to seek association in deviant peer groups (H*** B. Cantwell, "Child Sexual Abuse: Very Young Perpetrators," *Child Abuse and Neglect* 12 [April 1988]: 579-582).

THE FAMILY IN CRISIS

1. Constance Ahrons and Ray Rodgers, *Divorced Families: A Multidisciplinary Developmental View* (New York: W. W. Norton, 1987), 259; William J. Goode, *World Revolutions and Family Patterns* (New York: The Free Press, 1963), 432; Robert F. Winch et al, *Familial Organization: A Quest for Determinants* (New York: The Free Press, 1977), 259.
2. Ahrons and Rodgers, *Divorced Families: A Multidisciplinary Developmental View*, 259.
3. *Ibid.*, 259.
4. *Ibid.*, 259.
5. Ahrons and Rogers's conclusions about these changes in women's position in marriage are summed up in the following quotation: "As women become more independent economically their need for marriage as their source of economic support lessens. As they strive for more equality in society, their need for marriage as a source of status also lessens. Finally, when women may choose to have sexual relations without fear of pregnancy and societal scorn, their need for marriage as their only acceptable route to sexual satisfaction is reduced as well" (*ibid*, 14).
6. Harville Hendricks, *Getting the Love You Want* (New York: Harper & Row, 1988), 392.
7. Paul Bohannon, *Divorce and After* (Garden City, NY: Doubleday, 1970), 33-62.

8. A mounting body of opinion decries viewing divorce as pathological: Ahrons and Rodgers, *Divorced Families: A Multidisciplinary Developmental View*; Gay C. Kitson, Karen B. Barbric, and Mary J. Roach, "Who Divorces and Why," *Journal of Family Issues* 6 (September 1985): 255-294. The *Random House College Dictionary* defines pathology as "any deviation from a healthy, normal, or efficient condition" (New York: Random House, 1989). The idea is that the estrangement of divorce may be not so much a result of pathological personalities as two individuals who, when they relate, develop a pathological relationship. Roger L. Hutchinson and Sharon L. Spangler-Hirsch argue that research shows different but *not necessarily* disturbed patterns of development ("Children of Divorce and Single-Parent Lifestyles Facilitating Well-Being," *Journal of Divorce* 12 [January 1989]: 5-24). Other researchers seem to agree with my contention that both difference and disturbance are present: Robert S. Weiss, *Marital Separation* (New York: Basic Books, 1975); Judith S. Peck, "*The Impact of Divorce on Children at Various Stages of the Family Life Cycle*," *Journal of Divorce* 12 (December 1989): 81-106; Judith Wallerstein, "Children of Divorce: Preliminary Report of a Ten-Year Follow-Up of Young Children," *American Journal Orthopsychiatry* 54 (October-November 1984): 444-458.

9. Peck, *The Impact of Divorce*, 248.

10. Roberty Patton, Family Living, class notes from the East Tennessee State University course, Johnson City, TN.

11. Judity Wallerstein and Joan Kelly, *Surviving the Break-Up: How Children and Parents Cope with Divorce* (New York: Basic Books, 1980), 186.

12. Michael Nichols, *Family Therapy* (New York: Gardner Press, 1984), 351.

13. Julius Segal and Herbert Yahraes, *A Child's Journey: Forces that Shape the Lives of Our Young* (New York: McGraw-Hill, 1978), 354.

14. Marilyn J. Mason and Merle A. Fossum, *Facing Shame* (New York: W.W. Norton, 1986), 371.

15. John Bradshaw, *Bradshaw on: The Family* (Deerfield Beach, FL: Health Communications, Inc., 1987).

16. Mason and Fossum, *Facing Shame*, 116; Bradshaw, *Bradshaw on: The Family*, 39.

17. Mason and Fossum, *Facing Shame*, 172.

18. The following is an excerpt from Judy's Journal: "April, 1986 . . . My father sexually and physically abused my older sister more than any of us. In her adulthood, Cathy has told me that she felt angry at me because 'I got off easier' than she did . . . IT WAS NOT EASIER . . .. It was horrifying to stand helplessly by and witness her abuse, or that of my other sister, or more rarely, my brother. I felt enormous guilt and anguish whenever it was Kathy being hurt instead of me, I felt every blow emotionally just as surely as she felt them physically, I feel nauseated - sick to my stomach with outrage, helplessness, sorrow and grief. IT IS WRONG TO HURT CHILDREN . . . IT IS WRONG TO HURT PEOPLE! Whenever my sister was beaten, I stood stiff with fear, grateful it wasn't me, but afraid that at any moment he would turn on me. I scarcely dared to draw a breath. I remember my father sitting on top of my sister pinning her down, his leather strap raised to hit her, asking her where she wanted the welts this time - she had to pick. It makes me sick. My mother was there watching. SHE NEVER PRO-TECTED US FROM HIM. . .. She never tried to stop him, she never tried to help us. I wished with all my heart that my mother would take us away, would divorce him. She eventually did after 30 years, but by then I was married and a parent myself" (Robert Subby, *Lost in the Shuffle*, [Pompano Beach, FL: Health Communications, Inc., 1987], 42).

19. Brandt F. Steele, "Psychodynamic Factors in Child Abuse," in *The Battered Child*, 3rd ed., ed. C. Henry Kempe and Ray Helfer (Chicago: University of Chicago Press, 1980), Ray E. Helfer and C. Henry Kempe, eds., *The Battered Child* (Chicago: University of Chicago Press, 1968), 215-225.

RATIONAL DISCIPLINE

1. Parents may want to read more about RBT. There are several excellent and inexpensive books available. Two by Maultsby are: *Help Yourself to Happiness Through Rational Self-Counseling* and *Coping Better Anytime, Anywhere: The Handbook of Rational Self-Counseling*. The latter book is published by Prentice Hall (Englewood Cliffs, New Jersey, 1987), the former by the Institute for Rational Living, Inc. The local library will have Prentice Hall's address and ordering information. Readers may also write or telephone the Institute for Rational Living. The address and telephone number are: The Institute for Rational Living, Inc., 45 East 65th Street, New York, NY 10021, telephone (212) 535-0822. Ask the Institute about other related RBT and RET materials.

2. As originally reported by Albert Ellis, some nine clinically observed irrational ideas were frequently expressed by fifty-nine clients in his treatment population (Albert Ellis, "Outcome of Employing Three Techniques of Psychotherapy," *Journal of Clinical Psychology* 13 [October 1957]: 334-350). These were expanded to the current list of eleven that are now used by most practitioners of RBT and RET.

3. Maultsby refers to this sort of mental rehearsal as Rational Emotive Imagery (REI).

GETTING HELP

1. *"Most frequently asked questions about child abuse and neglect."* Unpublished material (Chicago, IL: National Committee for Prevention of Child Abuse, 1990).

2. J. A. Lewis, and M. D. Lewis. *Community Counseling* (Pacific Grove, CA: Brook Cole, 1989).

3. Thomas Holmes and Richard Rahe, "The Social Readjustment Rating Scale," *Journal of Psychosomatic Research* 11 (Winter 1967): 213-218.